Personal Ghost Stories

Stories

Volume One

Edited by
H.E. Bulstrode

CONTENTS

Foreword

Most people enjoy a good ghost story, even if they, like myself, should be of a distinctly sceptical cast of mind. It is a type of anecdote best enjoyed in company, the conviviality aided, perhaps, by the reader's beverage of choice, and the warmth of a real fire. As the nights lengthen, and the dampness and darkness of autumn give way to the chill of oncoming winter, our minds naturally gravitate towards the sleeping earth, and all the things that once were which now sleep within it, and may, just possibly, occasionally stir from their eternal slumber.

And so we come to the subject matter of this book: ghosts, hauntings, and kindred inexplicable phenomena, all of which might be gathered together under the heading of the 'supernatural'. To entertain the existence of such things, or, even worse, to admit to having experienced them, is frequently a source of embarrassment, and often an invitation to ridicule. Thus it is that the identities of the contributors have been concealed from the reader, for the sake of confidentiality. As to what ghosts and hauntings may be, that is a hoary old question indeed. Many answers have been suggested, with the most common being that they are but the fanciful figments of our imagination (there have, after all, been frauds and hoaxes aplenty). Even so, there are some who would aver that they have experienced things which defy logical explanation, and might, by the nature of their occurrence, merit the appellation of 'ghost' or 'haunting'.

There is an alluring charm to such stories, if not also, at times, a certain frisson of unease. But is that not what adds to the pleasure? And so, as you hold this book in your hands, huddled before your hearth, or lying in the warmth of your bed, what are you to expect of the pages that follow? A disparate mix, with some entries more detailed and polished than others; I am but their editor, having made nips and tucks to punctuation, paragraph structure and the occasional awkwardness of syntax, but nothing more. If you should find invention here, then it is not my own, and all that you see here has been reproduced in 'good faith', although I must own that I am no *gobemouche*. As to the sole inexplicable experience of my own which I have here related, I have done so faithfully and without embellishment. We are still puzzled by it to this day.

Each of the stories in this collection was freely volunteered for inclusion by members of the 'Personal Ghost Stories' Facebook group, with the events which they relate stated to have involved the contributor directly, or otherwise a close family member, or a friend. This book is dedicated to them.

Piano Lessons

I was maybe seven or eight at the time. It was in the 1960s when we lived in west London, and I used to take piano lessons in the house of two elderly ladies known as the Misses Reeves. They were spinster sisters: one was thin and the other was fat, and it was the larger of the two who tried to teach me piano in the front room of their little terraced house.

I was of an age when I was starting to feel my wings a bit, and was getting fed up and slightly insulted that my mother escorted me to the house only two streets away. I very much wanted to make the journey on my own. One sunny spring afternoon, I was standing ready with my music bag and shoes on, all in good time to go for my lesson. However, my mother was deep in conversation with a lady by the front gate, and was so absorbed that nothing could distract her.

I kept telling her it was time to go, but she shushed me away, and upon the third time of asking and getting rebuffed I just walked through the gate and went on my way, ignoring her angrily calling me back until I was halfway up the road.

At Number 13 Charles Street I was mildly surprised to find the 'wrong' sister opening the door to me, looking upset and red eyed. 'Oh no,' she said, 'you can't have your lesson today,' and I replied, 'But it's Tuesday,' and she said, 'Wait in the front room and I'll phone your mother,' (she'd actually have had to phone a neighbour as we didn't have a telephone until the seventies).

So I waited. I stood by the piano, and as the minutes went by I found that I was looking at myself in the mirror above the fireplace, through which I could see the staircase in the hall behind me through the open door. I could hear skinny Miss Reeves's voice as she made her phone call, but also saw fat Miss Reeves (sorry Miss Reeves) coming down the stairs in her green floral housecoat, clear as day with her hand on the banister. I turned round expecting to see her come into the room, but she didn't, and when I went back out into the hall skinny Miss Reeves said to me, 'You'd better go home, your mother's waiting for you.'

You can imagine with what dudgeon I walked home. My first attempt at independence had gone wrong, and I felt I had my tail between my legs. However, (I'm sure you know by now) Mum told me that she'd been calling me back because Miss Reeves had died that morning in her bed. And she wasn't impressed when I protested that she can't have died because I saw her coming down the stairs.

The Ghosts of Croome Court

When I left Kenilworth Castle I went to work for the National Trust at Croome in Worcestershire. I had an uneasy relationship with this property, and it is where some of my most terrifying experiences happened. But for now I will begin with one of the tamer tales from my time here.

Croome has an absolutely fascinating history, having evolved over the years from neo-Palladian mansion, to WW2 RAF base, to Catholic Boys School, to Hare Krishna UK headquarters, to failed hotel, to family home, before being bought by the Croome Heritage Trust in 2007 and leased to the National Trust.

I started in 2013 when the court was undergoing restoration work and much of it wasn't open to the public. I also therefore often found myself working in a huge, echoing mansion all alone. Although it quickly became apparent that you were never truly 'alone'.

One of the strangest experiences occurred in broad daylight in a room full of people. I was running a training session for new volunteers in one of the upstairs bedrooms that we'd repurposed as a meeting room. Once we'd finished the session one of the new volunteers approached me and asked if we had any costumed actors in the building. I said that we had done in the past for certain events, but not today.

'Why do you ask?' I said, and she replied, 'It's only because during your presentation I saw a lady in the doorway wearing an old-fashioned floor length dress.' She looked a little shaken.

I hadn't seen anyone in the doorway, nor had the rest of the group, but she was adamant that she'd seen a woman standing there.

'Do you think it might have been Barbara?' (the 6th Earl of Coventry's second wife), she continued. 'Only, because she appeared when you were talking about her.' I told her that Barbara wasn't known to be one of our restless spirits, but that the Earl's first wife, Maria, was often seen at this end of the house. As she seemed so unsettled I asked her if she'd ever seen anything like it before, and she shook her head.

I never encountered Maria myself, and I feel very thankful for that. Of all the ghosts in the court I felt the most uneasy about her. She had been a famous 18th-century Irish beauty, but her addiction to wearing heavy lead make up had ravaged both her looks and her health. She died at only 27, having essentially poisoned herself - a victim of cosmetics. She died at Croome in the bedroom opposite this same meeting room.

Though I never saw her, I often sensed her presence: never malevolent, just an overwhelming sense of sadness and loss that would wash over me at strange times at that end of the building.

Miss Kitty

It has been said that every English village has at least one ghost story, and the village in which I grew up proves to be no exception to this rule. What makes this one different however, at least for me, is the fact that this story involves my own family.

I grew up in rural Somerset, and the tale I am about to relate concerns certain occurrences in a house named 'The Laurels' which my parents rented almost forty years ago. Before proceeding, it is perhaps worth noting that both my father and I were of a distinctly sceptical frame of mind, whereas my mother and sister inclined towards indulging a belief in the supernatural. My mother was profoundly superstitious, and it was from her that we were fed the snippets of information relating to Miss Kitty that I outline for you below, for it was this woman whom she was convinced lay at the root of the disturbances at our then address.

Miss Kitty used to live in one of two cottages that had been demolished several decades earlier to widen the main road. One of these, I was led to believe, had once been the village smithy. In the years immediately following the last war, when my mother was a young girl, this lady was already of considerable antiquity, and had acquired a reputation amongst the locals as a witch. This was not a witch in the modern sense of the word, but a witch in the traditional understanding of the term: a woman of a sharp tongue, malicious character and dubious practices. As you might guess from her title, she was a single lady, a spinster whose character was not regarded with any degree of fondness. It was said that horses took an instinctive aversion to her, and were readily spooked by her presence. One driver who encountered her on the road one day found that his horse reared up in panic, threatening to overturn his trap, and it was only through a great effort of will that he was able to master control of the beast, which nonetheless refused to put another foot forward until the old woman had departed.

As to when Miss Kitty died, or how old she was when she did, I do not know. Neither do I know her surname, or the names of any of her relatives living or dead, but I do know that our landlady had something to say about her upon hearing of the experiences of my mother and my sister.

The house which we rented dated from the 1780s or thereabouts. It was a fair-sized dwelling, which back in the eighties was affordable even for a modest working-class family such as our own. To the rear of the property was a small yard with a disused well, safely capped by a stone slab, and to the front a cramped garden overlooking the main road. Its ground floor consisted of a lounge and a kitchen, with a sloping hallway which led down from the kitchen towards the stairs that ascended to the bathroom and four bedrooms spread over two storeys. My own bedroom was on the first floor, whereas my parents and sister slept in the two bedrooms on the storey above. We lived there for three years or so, and it must be said that it was not a happy time, particularly towards the end, when tragedy was avoided by a hair's breadth.

If I recall correctly, the strange happenings that occurred did so in our second year at the house, but they may have lasted for longer, for I experienced none of them, and it was only years later that my sister and mother revealed the full extent of the strange goings-on. They did make mention of some of these occurrences at the time, however, and I can remember that myself and my father derived a great deal of amusement from their reports, which is why they perhaps failed to mention many of the things that later came to light. One element that is consistent throughout, is that on no occasion when these happenings took place were either my father or myself present in the house; we were always elsewhere. It was as if whatever it was that lay at the root of these disturbances waited until my mother and sister were alone.

Nothing unusual was ever seen at our house, for the manifestations, if we may term them as such, were always either auditory, or olfactory in character. It was my younger sister who was the first to make mention of something out of place: the smell of burning candles in her bedroom, and neighbouring bathroom. There were no candles. This was a smell that was to recur on a number of occasions, usually in these two rooms, but sometimes in the short corridor that led to the small spare room and my bedroom on the first floor. I was not in the habit of burning candles. On other occasions my mother and sister would be sat talking in the kitchen, and would hear footsteps moving swiftly along the linoleum of the adjacent hallway, and someone running up the stairs. Sometimes the door to my bedroom, or to the neighbouring short corridor, would slam violently shut. They would muster up the courage to go upstairs, only to find that no one was there. Less frequently they might hear voices whispering in the hallway, which faded into nothingness as soon as they had been noticed.

On speaking to our landlady, my mother was informed that such occurrences had been reported by previous tenants, although we had never come to hear of them. She also revealed that at one time there was a communicating doorway from her own property to our house that had subsequently been walled up. Its position was at the end of the short corridor that led to my bedroom. Furthermore, she revealed that at one time Miss Kitty had resided there. It seemed to be her opinion, and that of my mother too, that the aforementioned village witch was wont to revisit her old home occasionally, and that she was the source of the phantom footsteps and inexplicable smells perceived about the house. It could have been, on the other hand, that the strange aromas had something to do with dodgy plumbing; that the phantom footsteps were nothing more than sounds transmitted through the floorboards of the blocked-off communicating corridor from our neighbours' house; and the slamming doors the mere consequence of open windows, gusts of wind and changes of air pressure within the house. For my mother and my sister, however, the preferred explanation was that it was Miss Kitty who was responsible.

By way of a coda, in recent years I was told that my father's new partner had one day gone to get her hair done in the village salon. Whilst there, she overheard a conversation between the hairdresser and one of her clients. The woman had not that long before moved into 'The Laurels', and she had a word or two to say about her new home. In sum, she wasn't altogether taken with it, as she and her family had found life there just a little unsettling. Why? Apparently for the very same reasons that my sister and mother never took to the place: strange sounds, smells and footsteps; the slamming of doors. Miss Kitty? I wonder. As to who lives there now, I've no idea.

Tommies on Princess Parade, Liverpool

For thirty years now, I have worked in the security industry, and have sometimes had the good fortune to work in some really interesting places.

My current position is on the Liverpool dockside, sometimes beautiful in the summer, but cold, windy and wet during the winter months. I have, however, been fortunate enough to witness some interesting happenings, both on the river, and on the dockside.

I was on a night shift when I saw them. The weather was fine; there was no wind, and it was quite a mild night as it was in the later part of the summer, so it stayed light for a good while.

I went outside for a cigarette about 02.20, looking around the area and taking in the beauty of the older buildings. I had been outside no longer than five minutes when I saw two figures walking from the direction of the Liver Building, and heading down Princess Parade as if heading towards the old dock road.

Being on security at the time, I stayed outside just to see where they were heading, and as they came nearer, I realised they were in uniform.

I recognised the uniform to be from the First World War, the puttees around the bottom parts of their legs being quite visible as the lighting is very good round that area. The uniforms were very clearly WW1.

Thinking that it was maybe just two people walking home from a fancy dress party, or some similar occasion, I just admired the way they dressed, only to realise they had weapons – rifles over the shoulders – and what looked like full marching order pack.

I stared on, and as they rounded the corner to head towards the dock road, both turned and seemed to acknowledge me being there. As they came to the small bridge crossing the canal, they vanished. I walked over in the general direction, but they were not to be seen: they had simply vanished.

I went back to my security post, put the kettle on to make a drink, and was suddenly seized by a sense of overwhelming sadness, which almost reduced me to sobbing. I went back outside to see if they could be seen, but they had gone.

I still work in the same area, and from time to time I will see the lads walking up. They seem to chat and be in high spirits, but each time they are seen, I still get that feeling of an overwhelming sadness.

Maybe they joined up and were killed, as so many were, or maybe the two friends were separated during the time they served, and never got the chance to meet back up. I would love to know their story, and to get a better understanding of why they walk this same path each time I see them.

A Fishy Tale of Thirsk

This happened many years ago when my in-laws lived in Lancashire. One day, after paying them a visit, we were returning back home and decided that we would stop at Thirsk for lunch. After arriving in the town, we parked our car, and not knowing the area decided to walk around to find somewhere to eat. We walked down a little side road where we came across a fish restaurant which looked quite promising. My husband was ahead of me when he suddenly stopped in the doorway. Naturally, as I was behind him, I bumped into him and asked him what the problem was. He pointed to a corner of the restaurant, and asked me if I could see a woman sitting there, and who I thought it might be. I confirmed that I did indeed see the woman who was tucking into a huge plate of fish and chips, and I told him it was his grandmother. Now, I must add that my husband's grandmother had passed away many years previously, so you would have thought that one of us would have picked up on this, but we didn't.

My husband stood stock-still, just outside the doorway, almost as if there was a barrier in the way and he could go no further. He gave me a knowing look and nodded, and suggested that we should go and look for somewhere else to eat before making our minds up. We did no more than head up to the top of the little road and look around the square, which took no longer than 10 minutes at the most, and as we couldn't find anywhere else decided to go back to the same restaurant where we had seen his grandmother. When we got there we once again looked inside, but the lady we had seen was nowhere to be seen. However, we went in and sat down next to the table where the lady had been sitting, and glanced over at where she had seated herself: her table was spotlessly clean; there was no evidence of anybody having been there, yet the person we both saw was as solid as solid can be. When the waitress came to take our order, my husband asked if anybody had recently been sitting at the table next to ours. She looked at us in bewilderment, and told us that nobody had been sitting at that particular table for several hours, whereupon we looked at each other. We were in a state of complete shock. Now, I can question my own sanity, but both of us saw the same woman that day. I knew it was my husband's grandmother, although I saw her sideways on. How? Because she ate in a very distinctive way, just as his grandmother used to; it looked as if her jaw became dislocated whenever she ate. I had no difficulty in identifying her. Even after all these years, if you asked either of us to relate this story separately without the other being there, the story is always the same.

The Hand on the Stairs

Ten years ago I was living in a beautiful old house in Clifton, Bristol. It was snug and cosy and charming, but at times a little eerie. I spoke with my then housemate, and we both agreed that we had sometimes caught what looked like movement out of the corners of our eyes, coming from the bottom of the stairs as we crossed the landing at the top.

Then, one hot and bright day, I was carrying a great pile of clean laundry out of the living room and turned to go up the stairs, when I distinctly saw a hand come out and grab for my ankles.

I yelped like a scalded thing, and all the laundry went flying everywhere as I instinctively went to slap the hand away. But of course there was nothing there. The house was quiet and some flies were buzzing over by the window.

Later, we had a friend to stay over who was pregnant. This friend refused point blank to climb the stairs at night, and the long corridor to the loo was a complete no-no. I ended up getting a small statue of Buddha to sit at the top of the stairs. He lent a calming presence to it all.

Not long after, I met the man who was to become my future husband. He told me he was a 'sensitive' and often saw things and people that were from other times and planes. For devilment, and because I'm eternally sceptical, I asked him if he had ever picked up anything in that house (bearing in mind that I had not yet told him of any of our experiences).

'Yes,' he said. 'There's a female presence in the house. She fell down the stairs and broke her neck, and now she's lying there, wondering why everyone is stepping over her, and no one is helping her get up.'

You can imagine how I became a little less sceptical after that.

The Visitor Who Brought His Own Ghost

I used to work on the desk at Farleigh Hungerford Castle in Somerset, which long ago fell into ruin, following the many misfortunes of the Hungerford family. It provides a home to a number of ghosts, including one often seen by people cleaning the museum cabinets in what was once the Great Hall. These glass cabinets are large, reaching almost to the ceiling, and it was while polishing these that a number of people claimed to have seen something very strange reflected in the glass: a tall, dark, jet black figure standing behind them. When they turned, they would find that there was no one there.

I would often discuss the supernatural while selling tickets, booklets and souvenirs to visitors. We had one regular visitor who was an older gentleman with a deep fascination for local history. He spoke in a very matter-of-fact way about how he often saw the ghost of a farmer in a smock driving a pig along the side of the road near Warminster. As if this were not unusual enough, he said that the farmer was visible only from his knees up, and as for the pig, only its backside could be seen. 'It's the same with them Romans,' he said. 'I have seen them Romans leaving a battle with the Dobunni (Iron Age tribe) on the (Somerset) Levels. Two either side of an injured man, hobbling along on the old Mark road.'

You can imagine standing in a haunted castle listening to this was quite something. 'But that ain't nothing,' he continued, 'my worst is the dairymaid.'

'Oh?' said I.

'She knocks on my front door at the farm, and when I answer she looks so cross with me. She just stands on the step staring at me with her yoke on and everything.'

'What do you do?' I asked.

'I just shut the door, but she follows me. It shakes me up.'

I did notice despite his cheery demeanour that he looked kind of nervous and shaken. 'I am sorry to say,' he said, looking behind him, 'that she is right here now.'

The Party at Margells

People have many different reasons for loving ancient buildings. For some, it's the magnificent craftsmanship and construction skills – so often using skills that are now increasingly difficult to find; for others, it's the integrity of the components. Many buildings have stood for centuries, and are constructed from nothing more than materials found locally, each possessing a unique quality and character that sets them apart from the generic structures which spring up today.

Yet for others, the reasons for their affection are less tangible. With interest in history as strong now as it's ever been, people love knowing more about a building's previous occupants. The details of their day-to-day lives can be just as enthralling as the architecture. For some buildings, such as palaces and stately homes, the research will be easy, with details of occupants, at least those above stairs, easy to find, whereas with many smaller, lesser houses hard facts are less easy to discover.

The availability of resources online has done much to enable the curious homeowner to discover the past, and there is one source of information, albeit unconventional, that if available promises to put flesh on the bones of what can be a very bare story. I am referring to the longstanding history of ghosts associated with ancient houses, especially those that may have been the scene of a bloody or traumatic event.

It was through my mother that I had any indirect experience with spectres. My mother Margaret and her sister Betty were visiting friends in Branscombe, East

Devon, around the time of the Second World War. Their stay was to be quite a lengthy one, and they quickly made friends with some local people.

My aunt was especially friendly with a chap called Terence who lived in a cottage west of the main village. His home, known as Margells, was thought to be the oldest house in the area. It was reputed to have belonged to a local abbey, prior to the Reformation, and to have been used as a retreat house for the monks.

This story is validated by a magnificent mediaeval wall painting still in evidence on a bedroom wall. Terence was a serious, hard-working young man not inclined to tell fanciful tales, yet he would often tell the story of Margells because it had moved him so much.

When he was a young man, his grandmother had come to live with them for her final years, and slept in a bedroom next to Terence's. For as long as he could remember, he had heard, just before going to sleep, muttering and murmuring that he attributed to his grandmother. Eventually, his grandmother died, but the sounds continued; every night he would hear the same noises. He told his father, since he was puzzled about the cause. His father told him the sound was always thought to have been the chanting of a monk. He said that someone had once witnessed a monk coming down the stairs with a bloodied bandage wrapped around his head.

Fast forward a few years and Terence took over running Potbury's, the local auction room, and Margells was sold to the Landmark Trust. When planning a holiday together, my mother and my aunt came across this information and booked it for a short stay. They were both aware of these stories, but being strong-minded brave women they dismissed these as rumours, relishing the chance to stay in such a beautiful building. But they hadn't been there long before unusual events had them puzzled. At first they heard footsteps going up and down the stairs, and pacing in empty rooms. The women put these unusual sounds down to the house's atmosphere. When the heavy cast-iron door knocker knocked of its own accord, they shrugged their shoulders and ignored it.

Not long afterwards they were surprised to hear a party going on in the house. They could hear laughter, chatter and the clink of glasses as if in celebration. The antics continued, with something that sounded like the lash of the whip striking between them. This time the couple couldn't ignore it, but all they could do was puzzle about the origins of the sounds and leave it at that. But they very strongly felt that if there was spirit in the cottage it wasn't malign, it simply wanted to be left alone.

It was their last night in the building that convinced the couple that the sounds they were hearing were emanating from a different era. By this time, both women were wary of possible spiritual occupants, and agreed to sleep in the two single beds in the same bedroom. They put the light off and lay down ready for sleep, but something kept them awake. After a while my aunt spoke, 'I wish you'd stop that snoring Margaret so I can get some sleep.'

My mother replied: 'I've been lying awake listening to that!'

The women froze as they realised there was no other explanation for the sound than a spiritual one. 'Leave us alone and we'll never come back here again,' called my aunt.

At that point, all noises stopped and the house was quiet for the rest of the night. The following morning the women left the cottage as agreed, totally convinced they had heard the spectre of a long-dead monk. Knowing my mother and aunt as down-to-earth women, these events convinced me that there just might be something otherworldly about some places.

Grasmere's Ghostly Footprints

For a while in the nineties, I lived with my ex-wife in the oldest house in the village, at the end of the road and at the top of a relatively remote valley in the Lake District. The house had once been an inn of some sort, being the last place to rest before heading up the drovers' road over into the next valley. It was very old: low beams, stone flagged floors, beautiful carved built-in oak vernacular furniture. It was a dream. Anyway, the front door was immensely old, made of oak and had a massive oak bolt on the inside. Once you were in, there was no need to lock the door, as all you had to do was simply slide this massive bolt across and you were secure. Immediately inside the door was a small entrance hall, stone flagged, with a solid wall in front, and doors to both the right and left. On the right was the sitting room, and on the left was the kitchen. So, to get to the kitchen from the sitting room, you had to cross this small hallway.

One evening after dark, we are watching a bit of TV and at the ad break I decided to make a cuppa. I opened the sitting room door to cross the hall into the kitchen, and when I did so I noticed a series of tiny footprints starting at the bolted front door, going over to the sitting room door, and then back again to the front door. Not only that, but they appeared to be on 'tip toes'. I looked at these prints, and called my wife over to have a look, and we both stood there puzzling over them for a minute or so. It was wet outside, and these were wet prints. Were they hers? To test whether this were so, she wet her feet and made a print next to them, and of course hers were much bigger. No, these were a child's footprints, and of course we had no kids and the door was bolted.

In 1992 we didn't have phones with cameras and didn't have any film for the old instamatic, and so we could not record them. As we stood scratching our heads, they slowly evaporated. We never did find a satisfactory explanation.

A Censorious Knock

An incident that intrigues me more than scares me happened in 2021 between COVID lockdowns. Myself and my girlfriend at the time liked to explore the countryside, looking at old churches, stone circles and other ancient sites around northeast Cumbria where I live. I'd heard of the abandoned village of Addingham in the Eden Valley, not far from the villages of Glassonby and Kirkoswald. Nothing is left of the village itself, as it was swept away by a flash flood, and then finished off by the Black Death in the Fourteenth Century. However, the Church of St Michael still stands alone in a field. It is a low solid building with an ancient Saxon wheelcross in the churchyard, and is still in use. That day, the door was open so we went inside, admiring the stained glass windows and ancient tombs built into the walls. Heading out back to the door we took advantage of the isolated location, and embraced in the doorway. As we held each other, we both distinctly heard singing, not chanting or hymns, but something more like an old folk song or nursery rhyme. It seemed to come from just outside the door, but it was indistinct and female. We broke off and listened. It lasted for no longer than perhaps 20-30 seconds, then stopped. We returned to what we'd been doing . . .

Then, from inside the church, possibly the vestry, two sharp knocks that sounded like wood hitting wood stopped us in our tracks. We looked around, but the atmosphere had changed; it had become ominous, darker somehow . . . perhaps some shade of a past parishioner or vicar disapproved of our moment of passion. Who knows? The singing could've been a walker I suppose, but we'd have heard them on the gravel path outside. The knocking could've been something falling off a shelf, but who, or what, had pushed it? What I can't explain is that atmosphere – so tangible, heavy and oppressive. Neither of us could explain it either at the time, or since.

The Widdowson Papers

When I left college in 1976, my first job was as a junior bank clerk in the Midland Bank, now HSBC, in Tunbridge Wells.

One lady who was near retirement had been there since she was 15, so she had been there for nearly 45 years. She knew everything there was to know about banking; knew the building inside and out. She was everyone's work aunty, as it were, and even the manager and accountant would defer to her incredible knowledge.

Sadly, due to the times, she had been passed over for management, but had got as high as a woman could in banking at the time. She was solid, practical and not given to fanciful flights of imagination, but she told us all a story that is very odd.

For the first twenty-odd years of her career an elderly customer called Mr Widdowson would come in every Friday at 9 a.m. to go through his papers and his security box for about an hour. Betty would escort him and, as was the policy, lock him in a small office in the basement next to the vault.

The same routine unfolded for twenty years until the final Friday that she locked him in with his box. Then, when she went to check on him . . . he wasn't there. His box sat on the table unopened. She promptly exited and sought out the other senior key holder, but was informed by the individual in question that they had been on the till all the time. Not only had no one let Mr Widdowson out, but neither had anyone seen him arrive or leave.

Betty then rang his home to ask if he had returned safely, and to explain that she must have forgotten to lock the office, only to be told by his son that Mr Widdowson had died a few days earlier.

The Vanishing Man in a V-Neck

I live in the Scottish Borders, an area steeped in ghostlore, haunted houses, castles and lonely roads. One such road is the A75 just north of Annan, known as the Kinmount Straight.

However, my experience is further south in the village of Dornock, just over the border east of Annan. One evening in November 2013, driving towards Annan to pick up a former girlfriend's daughter from dance class, we were driving through the village slowly due to icy roads and a lack of street lighting, when I noticed a figure standing at the side of the road. Nothing unusual in that, I thought, until the figure stepped into the road to cross in front of the car. The figure was definitely male, and was wearing a red V-necked jumper and dark trousers, but appeared somehow indistinct in the headlights as we slowed to let him pass. He walked casually in front of the car, but didn't reach the other side of the road.

I asked my partner if she had seen the figure, and she said that she had, and remarked that he must've walked into one of the houses. I replied that if he had done he must've walked through a hedge, as we'd have seen him walk past the car on the opposite side of the road. But we had seen nothing. He must've gone somewhere, surely?

We drove on to pick up her daughter, but I realised later that we'd gone the long way around to our house at Canonbie, adding an extra 20-30 minutes onto our journey instead of driving back through Dornock. Something subconsciously made us go the long way around. I've no explanation for this. A few months later, I read a post on Facebook from a local ghost-hunting group called *Mostly Ghostly* that mentioned the famous Kinmount Straight, and stories attached to it, as a footnote. Dornock was referenced in a story about a woman in a Victorian dress standing near a railway bridge. It also mentioned, however, another figure: a man in relatively modern clothing wearing a red V-necked jumper who had been seen near the church, watching cars before stepping into the road and vanishing.

The Bothy

For a number of years, I worked as an educator/tour guide at an historic property. One old building, The Bothy, had housed the garden staff in Georgian times; they were of a range of ages, from young boys to grown men, all living, eating and sleeping there. In the present day it was used as a classroom for visiting school groups. I loved working in there. I never felt alone; there was always a strong sense of being watched, but not in an unpleasant way. Little things would happen, too – nothing major, just hats popping off pegs in front of you; things coming unpinned from notice boards as you looked at them; stopped clocks chiming. I developed a habit of greeting the residents in the morning as I came in – 'Morning gentlemen. How are you today?'

My strangest experience came while setting up tables for a school party, laying out equipment that included felt tip pens. One area of the bothy had a significant slope to the floor, so the table there was on quite a slant. I laid out three sets of equipment on the table and was about to move on to the next, when one of the felt pens suddenly rolled across the table - UP THE SLOPE. I stared at it in disbelief for a moment, then put it back - and it did the same thing again. *Oh really!* I thought. I felt a bit irritated now, and found myself standing there with my hands on my hips and my head tilted, glaring at the pen rather in the way I glare at my children when they have been caught out up to no good. I moved the pen again, and it rolled back again. After about five attempts to get the pen to behave I gave up. I said, 'Sorry lads, I haven't got time for this,' and carried on setting up the rest of the session, pretty sure that a cheeky eighteenth-century pot boy had been having a good old joke at my expense.

The Shed on the Allotment

An old lady I used to visit as a patient back in my NHS days told me a story about an allotment that she and her husband used to walk past on their weekly stroll after attending church on a Sunday morning. She said that they had walked past it one particular Sunday back in the eighties, and had noticed in the corner of the allotments a broken-down old shed surrounded by overgrown weeds. They were not surprised to see it looking in such a state, as it had been like that for many years, but as they walked past they were both surprised to see a new-looking shed in its place, which was surrounded by beautiful flowers and plants. Outside was a blonde-haired lady smoking a cigarette in a holder of some sort, and dressed in a style from the forties or fifties which they kind of remembered. She said they didn't think much about it other than to comment to each other how good it was for that corner of the allotment to be cared for again. On their return about an hour later, they were taken aback to see that it had reverted to its old neglected state again. She said that had they both not witnessed it she would have thought she had imagined it. The lady was totally sane by the way, and not prone to telling fibs.

A Pinch in Time

Around ten years ago,[1] I took a group of children to Clarke Hall in Wakefield.[2] The hall used to allow the children, dressed in appropriate outfits, to experience a day as a Tudor. We split the children into groups, and I was stationed in the dining room. The two members of staff were in authentic dress and briefed the teachers on the activities and historic details in each room. A staff member went off up the stairs with my group of children, and then was supposed to return with the next set. I waited alone downstairs. After a few minutes, I saw him walk past the windows in the garden and across the lawns. I was a little annoyed by this, as I had been left waiting for the children and was concerned that they would miss out on time to complete the activities we had planned.

Just as I was about to text my TA upstairs, the children were led down and into the dining room. At lunchtime the curator asked if everything was all right as I looked quite shocked when he brought the children in. I said yes, that it was just that I hadn't realised that three of them were working in costume today, and that I saw the other man outside. He went very quiet and simply responded that only he and the cook worked there, and the gate to the rear garden was securely locked for safety.

---

[1] 2011 or thereabouts.
[2] Formerly in council ownership, but now in private hands. A three-year survey revealed the house, thought to be Elizabethan, to have been extensively remodelled during the latter part of the 1670s.

Later that afternoon, as we were watching the children learn a Tudor dance, a friend was standing with her back to the fireplace/priest hole. I noticed how she edged away and around to the window instead. She looked concerned. I made my way over to her thinking she had spotted the children possibly 'up to something,' but she simply said she would tell me on the bus. We continued to watch the dancing when we both suddenly jumped and squealed. Everyone looked at us, and I just said we got a fright from a spider. In fact, we had both been grabbed on the bottom. She later told me that she had moved from the fireplace as something had stroked her face and hair. We were asked if we had squealed due to the spider, or *something else*. They were, it seems, aware of the presence of an overly-friendly spirit in that room.

Strange Occurrences at Kelmscott Manor

I work as a volunteer at Kelmscott Manor, Oxfordshire, once home to William Morris and his family. It is a house with a distinctive Cotswold character and charm, possessing a long history dating back to the Elizabethan era; just the sort of place, in fact, that you think would harbour a ghost or two, although when I started there I had not heard mention of any haunting.

It was 10.30 one fine May morning last year,[3] half an hour or so before the manor opened to the public. I was sitting in Kelmscott's kitchen quite alone, and having decided that I could put off the call of nature no longer, I took myself off and popped to the loo. To get there, I

[3] May 2022.

had to pass out of the modern kitchen and through the old one, but just as I got to the toilet something rather unexpected happened: there was a loud shout in my ear: 'Boo!'

You can well imagine how startled I was. Instinctively, I cast a glance back over my shoulder, only to discover that there was no one there. It really was very strange, and yet I felt in no way discomfited by this sudden and unexpected exclamation, despite there being nowhere that anyone could have hidden; but that I had heard this shout I had not the least doubt. As you can imagine, it left me feeling as if something else might happen, but beyond that single 'boo!' nothing else out of the ordinary occurred.

Who, or what, was it? I don't know, but I do know that there seemed to be no malice in it, for it was rather a good-humoured 'boo!' When I mentioned it to the manager afterwards, they didn't seem to have heard of anything of the like taking place there before. However, I have heard of at least one other strange occurrence in this historic house, which took place out of hours in the bedroom that used to be slept in by William Morris. A staff member was inside talking to a conservator when one of its doors suddenly closed. It came as quite a surprise, for it had been left ajar, and no one else was in that part of the house at the time. When the conservator tried to open the door, which opens inwards, it was found to be stuck fast, as if someone were pulling it from the other side. Having tried, and failed, to open the door several times, the final pull saw it fly open only to reveal an empty landing; unexpected, of course, as was the fact that the force which had previously been applied from the other side of the door had ceased in an instant.

This particular incident occurred shortly after a multi-million pound renovation project that was carried out whilst Covid was at its height in 2020. Just as was the case with my own unusual experience, neither of the two individuals felt uneasy about what had happened. Whatever had been playing with them would appear to have been doing just that: playing. It seems to have been an unusually benign and friendly spirit.

Mrs Puddinghead

Firstly, I should tell you that this really is a 'true' ghost story; I could write up other odd experiences that I have had over the years, but all of them could, and, probably do, have perfectly logical explanations . . . this one too, I suppose, if you look at it from the viewpoint of a stern rationalist. And if you didn't experience it yourself.

I'm also happy to admit right at the start that I may be the least psychic person in the UK. I could sleep quite soundly and happily in some allegedly haunted rooms, and, not see, hear or intuit a thing. Perhaps that makes it all the odder that this incident has stayed with me so vividly all these years. Anyway, here is the story.

In 1986, I was at college in Canterbury. Now, any city that can boast a 900-year-old cathedral - the site of the brutal murder of an Archbishop in 1170 - a town full of wild and sinister stories, lonely corners and strange lore, has a certain eldritch charm, not to mention a spooky reputation to uphold. However, it wasn't in any of those particular dark lanes that I had my encounter with what I think of as a ghost.

At this time, I was living with two friends, as the houseguests of an elderly man, John Weekley, who would let students stay with him, completely rent free, for a term or two, just for a bit of company. The only downside was that John's bungalow was in a tiny village called Westbere, about 6 miles outside the city walls; not too much of a problem though, when balanced against all that rent money to be saved.

To get to and from college I could hitch a lift, or jump on a bus. I could even, if I had drunk enough at the student bar to insulate myself from the cold, or was feeling particularly energetic, walk all the way home, and sometimes did, although this meant walking alone down an unlit road past the village church and graveyard.

Our sort-of semi-landlord, John, with his monocle and plus fours, was a real character; despite his age, he was amazingly active. Most days he would call for a taxi to take him into Canterbury to spend the afternoon at the Shakespeare Arms in Butchery Lane. It was only later that we found out the reason he had to go so far afield for his regular pint: at the age of 84 he had been banned for life from the village pub for raucous behaviour.

Having lived in the village all his life, John was full of the most hair-raising stories - like the time he claimed to have run into the Headless Horseman of Margate, and what it was like to have been in Canterbury during the brutal Baedeker bombing raid of 1942, when the High Street was strafed with machine gun fire by the Luftwaffe. In fact, John, who rarely stopped to draw breath, was a real fount of all local knowledge.

Oh, and before I forget to tell you, there was one thing, and one alone that John forbade us to do: unless it was a case of the most dire emergency, we were not allowed to use his telephone. But, as there was a red phone box at the village end of the lane, this wasn't really a problem.

Even in those long ago, pre-mobile phone days, I tried to make sure of calling my parents once a week, so every Sunday night, armed with plenty of loose change, I would dawdle up to use the telephone box.

The other end of Walnut Tree Lane was a dead end, terminating in a pretty white cottage by the side of the railway line that ran behind our house. In those days, if you were brave or foolhardy enough to take a shortcut and pick your way across the train tracks, you would find yourself in a nature reserve, made after the closure of some gravel pits.

At the time of my story, it was the fag end of autumn. You could sense the impending winter, for it was the sort of frosty November night where you can see your own breath and feel your cheeks reddening and tingling from the cold. I had made my weekly phone call, and was heading back to the warmth of the bungalow.

The street lamps had just come on and were glowing gold. I was feeling quite relaxed. I remember looking forward to getting back indoors and making myself a hot drink. There were footsteps coming towards me, heels clicking on the tarmac. Being a no-through road meant that the lane was usually deserted after dark. I looked up to see who else was out on such a raw night, expecting to see a dog walker, or one of our neighbours.

Coming up the lane was a woman I didn't recognise. She was warmly buttoned up in a brown winter coat. Like me, she was wearing glasses, and she also wore a hat - a sort of turban affair wrapped around her dark hair.

She looked perfectly normal, but as soon as I set eyes on her, I could almost feel my flesh shrinking away in an overwhelming repulsion. I could not bear the thought of her passing close to me. I have never felt so strongly repelled by anyone, or anything, before or since that night.

Some strange instinct took over and, without even thinking, I hared up the road towards her, turning off and running down our driveway just before we crossed paths. I flung myself so hard in through the kitchen door that the next day I found bruises on my arm.

Breathless, I listened. The woman's footsteps continued past the house and up the road. Now I was safely inside, the fear I felt had completely evaporated, leaving me feeling utterly foolish - what had come over me? I must have looked a complete idiot. Too embarrassed to tell anyone what had happened, I more or less forgot about the incident, and my trips to the telephone box continued as before.

The term ended. Eventually Spring arrived, and with the coming of lighter evenings, I even grew blasé about walking home alone past the graveyard. One day, after I had taken a long walk around the nature reserve, I returned home to find John gearing up to tell us some of his stories. He filled his pipe and took a few puffs. We settled down with a cup of tea and waited patiently to hear what fantastical bit of old puffery he was going to come up with this time.

A lot of time has passed, and John is long gone, but to the best of my remembrance, this is the gist of one of the stories that he told us that evening.

In the early days of World War Two, John and his family were living in a house a little further in towards the centre of the village. He and his missus had two young daughters, and these girls were fast friends with the children of the couple who lived in the white railwayman's cottage at the far end of the lane.

One day, this boy and girl came home from school to find that there was nobody home to let them in, no sign of life, no smoke coming out of the chimney.

Not knowing what to do, they circled the house, tapping at the windows, before eventually walking down to the Westbere Arms, to ask for help. The publican fetched the local bobby, and, together with a few other stout lads, leaving the children in the warmth of the pub with a glass of pop each, the men went back to their home and managed to break in the kitchen door.

A grisly sight confronted them: the railwayman had killed his wife, then cut his own throat. It was rumoured locally that the family had had grave financial problems and it was these that had led the man to commit this terrible act.

John paused dramatically. Taking his time, he tamped down his tobacco, and re-lit his pipe. Then he continued. Did we know that the murdered woman was supposed to haunt the lane outside? He hadn't actually seen her himself, but knew plenty who claimed they had.

Then he added, rather gleefully, a little bit of character assassination. Although the neighbours had liked the man, the locals had never really warmed to his wife; for a start, she was from London, and, as if this wasn't damning enough, it was also generally agreed that she gave herself airs and graces. For example, many of the villagers disapproved behind her back of what they considered as her inappropriately modish way of dressing; even though she made her clothes herself, they were always cut in the very height of fashion.

However, it was the unruly village children who used to be the real bane of her life, frequently running after her in the street shouting, 'Mrs Puddinghead,' because of the highly fashionable turban that she insisted on wearing, even out in the middle of the English countryside.

Daisy, Daisy . . .

I have a strange but true story which you may find interesting. When giving birth to my son, things were not going well. I was not on pain relief, just gas and air. I hallucinated a man with a sack on his back in the room. I asked the midwife who he was.

Fast forward a couple of years. When my eldest son was little he would tell us he was visited by Tom and his dog. Thomas is my son's middle name, but he was named after my husband's grandfather. He said he had a sack of black rock. Thomas was a coalman. I never met or saw a picture of Tom, so can't say if that is who I saw. My son told us that Tom had a baby but wouldn't let him come and live with us as 'it wasn't time'. After a while he stopped mentioning Tom, and as we could not have more children we thought no more of it.

Seven years after the birth of our first son, I was extremely surprised to have a second child. The pregnancy had been difficult with no heartbeat detected on several occasions, and when the baby was born he was blue and cold and had to be resuscitated. One afternoon, I put him in the crib for a nap and went to the kitchen. I could hear a girl's voice on the monitor. I thought it was a signal problem. I went to the bottom of the stairs carrying the monitor, and could hear the baby giggle on both the monitor and from his room, but only hear the girl on the monitor. I ran upstairs thinking we had an intruder in the house. Nobody was there. That night was the first time we called the ambulance because he stopped breathing. We only got to him in time because we could hear the girl's voice shouting 'Mum! Mum! Dad!' on the monitor. My husband ran upstairs and found him blue. This happened several times until his second birthday when they operated.

Things would move around the house, there were strange noises and my elderly aunt (92) would ask why we brought Daisy to visit when we went there. She said she was the same age as our eldest son, and had long curly red hair. If our youngest is going to be ill, I know it's coming even though he is seventeen, because Daisy always turns up first.

A Posthumous Farewell

Nine years ago a person very special to me passed away. We were the closest of friends, and although we were not attached romantically, we loved each other. We always said we were soul mates. He had moved to Cambridge years previously, but, thanks to social media and Skype, we were still in close contact. I knew he had an incurable lung condition, but he'd coped with it for so long that it didn't seem a threat. Sadly, over the course of six months or so, he deteriorated rapidly. I desperately wanted to see him, but found it so difficult to arrange, as I have an autistic son who cannot cope with travel. So, we kept in touch as much as possible in our usual way. I woke one morning with the absolute knowledge that he had died, only to have this confirmed a couple of hours later, when his daughter rang to tell me the sad news.

During the last week of his illness, he told me that he would come to me and let me know he was there. A few days after his death, I woke early and I was so overcome with sorrow that I was sobbing like a baby. At that moment, I felt his hand on my cheek, just as he used to do. A moment later I heard my purse, which has two cat bells attached, jingling inside my handbag. Later that morning, I came home from shopping and made myself a cuppa. Sitting down in the living room, I was shocked to see a candle on the hearth was burning. It hadn't been burning earlier, and there was nobody else in the house at all. This scared me, because I was worried that the cat or dog could have knocked it over and caused a fire while I wasn't there. I told him I loved the fact that he had come to me, just as he said he would, but I asked him to please not light a candle again. I still think of him often, but nothing has happened to suggest he has ever visited me again.

Nanna

In the late nineties, when I was a university student, I lived in a typical Australian student share house. The house was a rambling old place with several bedrooms, a kitchen, two lounges and a bathroom. A big backyard with a table tennis table in it completed a pretty nice set-up.

There was some furniture left over from the previous owner and a few boxes of old magazines.

It was common knowledge that it was allegedly haunted by an old lady who had lived her entire life in the house and had died in my bedroom (lucky me).

I was sharing the house with three girls and a guy, and quite often late at night we could hear what sounded like someone walking round the house checking that the doors and windows were locked and the house was secure.

Being students, we always assumed that it was another one of the housemates trying to being funny, but no one ever owned up to it.

Someone suggested that it must be the ghost and that we should just let it be. From then on, whenever something strange happened, we put it down to 'Nanna' as we christened her, and tried hard to made her feel as welcome as possible.

Some of the old magazines in the boxes were *TV Week* with various game shows circled so we put what was clearly the old lady's favourite chair in prime position in front of the TV, and made sure that we put the game shows on if we were home.

We set a place for her at our dinner parties, made sure the house was locked and always said hello when we came home and good night before going to bed.

Our house and 'Nanna' became quite well known at our university, and lots of people were keen to come over and sit in 'Nanna's chair'. Funnily enough, they always seemed to lose their nerve.

All of us felt quite protective of her if we felt a visitor was making fun of her, and more often than not, they were quickly shown to the door.

We never felt threatened or watched or even slightly uneasy in the house, quite the opposite in fact. It was almost like a warm blanket of reassurance every time you came home.

We could still hear her doing her nightly check-up, but none of us ever saw her.

The year ended and most of us were graduating and moving on. The happy house we had was breaking up so we decided that we should all head out for a night on town to celebrate a wonderful year.

We booked a taxi for 8 p.m. and opened the front door, leaving the security door closed.

The girls went to get ready, while we boys went to the backyard for a game of table tennis and a beer.

Then 8 p.m. came and the taxi arrived and sounded its horn. The girls were still getting ready and we weren't paying much attention in the backyard, so before any of us could get to the door, the taxi drove off.

Obviously we were a bit annoyed at this and had a bit of a go at the girls for not being ready. They, quite rightly, fired back that we too should have been paying more attention.

Ten minutes later, we were on the phone to the cab company to order another cab when the doorbell rang. Opening the security door, we found a cab driver. We asked him if he had just been to the house and his answer still makes the hair on the back of my neck stand up.

'I got here about ten minutes ago but the old lady behind the screen door told me you weren't quite ready and asked me to return in 10-15 minutes.'

We decided not to go out that night, instead the five of us sat in the main lounge and had a few drinks with 'Nanna' to thank her for making us so welcome in what was obviously still her home.

A Cumbrian Curiosity

Now the time has finally come to tell a tale that is true. As to whether you should think it a ghost story, or to have something of the supernatural about it, I shall leave entirely up to you. And it took place a few years ago when my wife and I took an October break in the Cumbrian village of Bampton, a small place with no great claim to fame, other than its old red telephone box which features in a memorable scene from the cult film *Withnail and I*. In this, Withnail, played by Richard E. Grant, engages in a futile foul-mouthed tirade against his ineffectual agent back in London. Unlike Withnail, however, we had not come here on holiday 'by mistake'. And, luckily for me, Uncle Monty was not in tow.

The weather during our stay was characteristically appalling. With the fells being strictly off-limits, we found ourselves largely confined to our holiday apartment, reading and writing whilst the wind howled and the rain lashed without. But on the Sunday afternoon there was a brief lull between the storms. Donning waterproofs and stout boots, we set off to walk to the neighbouring village of Bampton Grange whilst the light yet allowed. We saw no others on the few hundred metres of tarmac flanked by grey drystone walls that link these two fragments of this scattered parish, and had we not been on holiday, I doubt that we would have chosen to venture out either.

We crossed the old stone bridge over the River Lowther, beneath which rushed its waters bloated and black, anticipating the pleasures of the warmth of a roaring hearth in the village pub, only to find it closed for the season. In our disappointment we cast our eyes about, and there opposite they alighted upon the village church - St Patrick's. It was an unassuming looking place, neither particularly old, nor particularly new, but as it happened to be unlocked we decided to step inside. The gales had abated, but the wind was still brisk, so we took care to secure both the outside and inside doors behind us. It was calm and gloomy inside, the air cool and damp, heavy with the quintessential mustiness of an English parish church.

We found ourselves quite alone in this unremarkable space, and searched it high and low for items and features that might pique our interest, finding but little other than a list of the previous incumbent rectors of the parish, pondering as to why there were a number of gaps: the Black Death? The Interregnum? We kissed. And then—

Our moment was interrupted by the distinctive sound of the lift and fall of the iron latch of the outer door, and the muffled noise of someone fussing in the entrance beneath the bell tower. Almost guiltily we broke from our embrace, and instinctively looked in the direction of the inner door. The upward click of its latch then sounded, and its covering drapes billowed inwards. There was a pause, after which the drapes fell quite still. No one entered. And whereas we had heard the upward movement of the latch quite distinctly, we did not hear any corresponding downward rattle or clunk. The church had fallen into a total silence. Beyond the door we could hear nothing. I at once walked over and pulled it open, only to find the space beneath the bell tower empty. The outer door was closed as we had left it. Given the heaviness of this other door and its latch, it struck us as odd that anyone could have opened and closed it without making a sound. I walked over and opened it in turn, so as to look out down the church path. No one.

We decided to leave, but upon my return to close the inner door I found it to be stuck fast. No matter how I exerted myself, it simply would not close. So, I then did the logical thing, of course, and checked inside to see if it had snagged on the curtains. It had not, and neither were there any other visible obstacles to account for its stubborn refusal to shut. I tried again. No luck. No matter how hard I tugged, it simply would not budge. I tried a third time, but still to no effect; I just could not shut that door. Then came my fourth attempt. No sooner had I lifted the latch, than the door slammed shut with an unanticipated violence, as if it had been pushed with great force from within. I had not exerted so much as an ounce of effort to pull it. On no other occasion have I felt my spine tingle as I did at that moment.

As I have made clear, other than ourselves there had been nobody else in that church, and yet its door had been slammed in my face. We looked at each other and left without further pause, closing the outer door behind us without any issue. I glanced back only the once as we exited along the church path, but saw nothing out of the ordinary. We returned the following day to take another look, but found the church to be locked. And whereas on a number of occasions subsequent to our visit I have sought to ascertain whether anyone else has experienced anything of a like nature in St Patrick's Church, Bampton Grange, I have to date drawn a complete blank.

A Hat Trick

This account was given by a family friend. It's not a ghost story but is quite bizarre.

The background to this is that the lady that gave the account was a very 'matter of fact' person, quite stern in fact, not prone to fanciful stories or pulling people's legs.

We happened to be talking of strange events one day (the friend, my grandmother, mother and I). I was only a child so just sat listening.

The friend recounted that one day, she was in the family home when her husband returned. The house was unremarkable and neither of them had ever experienced anything out of the ordinary there. It was his habit to throw his hat onto a hat/coat stand in the far corner of the room. I forget how far away she said it was, but it was some distance and was a source of amusement to them that he rarely missed the peg. On this day he threw his hat as usual but half way across the room it vanished and never landed on the peg. They were astounded, both having seen it happen. They searched the room thinking that somehow they had been mistaken, but the hat was gone and they never found it. They could never explain what had happened to the hat. She didn't believe in ghosts and the supernatural, but knew that she had witnessed something inexplicable.

I have wondered since if somewhere in the world, in the same instant, a hat dropped out of thin air.

A Step in Time in a Pennsylvanian Farmhouse

In the year I was ten, my family moved to Pennsylvania. The house was built in 1768, and had several additions built over the years. My room was in the original part of the house - the two windows at the top, which looked out over empty fields to a distant line of dark forest.

I don't know whether it is a trick of the age I was, or if the house itself etched the year so deeply into my memory - that I can recall every day as clearly as if I am still there. I can close my eyes and walk through the rooms, look out the windows, and it is all perfectly vivid and true. I often run through the past just before sleep - this is where I go. I was completely happy there.

My mom woke in the night about a month after we arrived. She heard me walk down the hall, past her door, on my way to the bathroom. She knew it was me because it was a light, slippered footstep. She waited for me to pass again, and when I didn't return, got up to check. I was asleep, my brother was asleep, and as she climbed back into her own bed, dad rolled over and asked what she was doing.

'You're going to think I'm crazy - but somebody just walked down the hall.'

Dad said, 'It must have been the cat.'

The cat was outside.

Then the footsteps walked back down the hall.

As mom tells it, 'Your dad got out of bed like his tail feathers were on fire.'

They turned on all the lights and walked through the house top to bottom. Mom thought it was me. I think of this sometimes - and wonder.

We got used to the idea that we were not entirely alone, fairly quickly - and referred to the other one as 'she'. Always a soft footfall, accompanied by a sweet, smokey scent - like a trail of perfume you would walk through, turn - and it was gone.

We all had our encounters. Always thinking it was somebody in the family - only to be surprised when it was not.

Sitting in the kitchen one afternoon doing my homework, my little brother walked slowly down the long flight of stairs around the corner. Except he never entered the kitchen. I was alone in the house.

Well . . . maybe not?

'She' only walked in the old part of the house. The bathroom at the end of the hall was a later addition - and it's as if these areas didn't exist for her. It seemed to me then that someone who lived here a very long time ago, still loved the house and stopped by to make sure it was all OK.

Sitting around one bright Sunday afternoon, lying on my tummy on the living room rug reading the funny pages - mom jumped up and charged across the room. The electrical wiring was old, and the floor socket behind the wing chair must have shorted out - as there was a column of smoke rising by the right side of the fireplace.

Only about five feet high, but as we all watched - it folded in on itself, and disappeared.

The single year's rental came to an end, and we met the family who had just bought 'my' house. They were from New York – two boys (the eldest being my age), new baby, mom, dad, and mother-in-law – and trooped through the rooms, peering into the corners, as I was tasked with showing the brothers the barn.

They were going to make big changes. Dad already had plans for tearing out the old spring house, and putting in a swimming pool. I hated them on sight.

The day we left, I cried my way through the empty rooms, and vowed that 'When I am all grown up, I will buy you back and will come home to live here forever.' I wondered how 'she' would feel about those boys and their new swimming pool.

Two years later. The morning newspaper had a photo of the burned out shell of a stone farmhouse in Pennsylvania. Half of the front wall still standing, two windows at the top, and the leaning tower of a chimney - everything else was gone. Standing outside the striped plastic tape of the perimeter, the sound of the wind as it came through my bedroom windows - the smell of the smoke and the shivering cold of a January day in 1969 - remains shard-sharp.

The story told in the paper - the dad was away on a business trip when the fire started out by the pool house and travelled up the new breezeway to the house itself. Because the nearest neighbours were a farm five miles away, nobody noticed until it was a light in the night sky.

Mom, both boys, the baby, and mother-in-law were found by the front door after the ceiling collapsed over them.

Is it alright if I believe that a small part of me died with them? And so . . .

I have spent a lifetime since that distant year, and visit in my dreams; still vivid in its infinite detail. The evening light falls through the wavy glass of the windows, and drifts across the dark wood of the far wall. I can step into the huge fireplace in the sitting room, and stand looking at the square patch of blue sky high overhead. I curl up on the wide window seat and look out across the stubble of winter corn fields under a low grey sky.

More real than my actual present days . . .

Here is my question. When my mother rolled over that first night to hear footsteps walking past her door - she was completely certain that it was me. I am haunted by the notion that in some mysterious way, perhaps it was. A time slip off to one side - and I slide between the cracks?

I loved the house of my memory, and visit frequently. Has it been me all along?

The Man in White

I heard this a long time ago from my mum. When she was a child, her brothers sometimes played outside late in the fields. One night, my mother's brother, Bill, was playing with his friend and realised the time was later than they thought. It was dark and he and his friend decided to take a short cut across a piece of land, where they happened to be building some new houses. When Bill arrived home, he was in a terrible state, crying and clearly traumatised. It turned out that as they were passing the new houses, a figure all dressed in white had crossed in front of them and gone into one of these houses. My grandmother finally calmed Bill, not very convincingly, by telling him that it could have been a workman in overalls, back to get some paint. Anyway, time passed and the houses were finished. The one the strange man went into, was given to a miner. But he only lived in that house three weeks before he was killed down the pit. Odd eh?

The Vanishing Cyclist

This actually happened to me just eight years ago. I live in southwest Missouri – the Ozarks – and have for most of my life. I have two sisters who now live in NW Arkansas, an area that we are all very familiar with and have travelled back and forth between all of our lives, day and night. I say that because it's an important detail.

There is an area just south of the Missouri state line as you enter into northwest Arkansas and must travel through before you get to the more populated area where my sisters live; it's very rural, and happens to be the home of Pea Ridge Military Park where the Battle of Pea Ridge was fought during the Civil War. Up until just a few years ago the main two-lane road went right by the military park entrance/visitors centre. It has since been bypassed by a four-lane highway, but there still aren't many houses or businesses along the new highway.

Anyway, one night I had been visiting one of my sisters as I often do, had dinner and hung out a while, then began the drive back home to Missouri . . . usually about an hour and a half to two hour drive. It was already dark and getting late, but I preferred that since there was less traffic.

When you approach the military park it's very dark, cell phone service would drop off, there are no street lights, and you had to watch for deer ALWAYS. As I began to approach the military park on the highway I saw something moving to the right up ahead that my headlights had picked up. As I got closer I could see it was someone riding a bicycle (this all happened very fast). As I got even closer, and pulled slightly to the left to go around as there was no oncoming traffic, I looked over and could not believe what I was seeing. There was a young man riding an old Penny Farthing bicycle (I think that's what they're called, the huge wheel in front that sits way high up off the ground) and I think he had a pageboy cap on, although I do not recall seeing a face. It was there clear as day and I was stunned that anyone would be riding ANY kind of bike down that highway between 9 and 10 p.m., much less an old bike like that.

I went around and looked in my rear-view mirror, watching the image fade from sight and still marvelling at what I had just seen. My instinct was to call my sister and tell her what had just happened, but I had no service until I got closer to Missouri. To this day, I know what I saw but I cannot explain it.

Another odd aspect was that I could see him clearly though there were no streetlights and my headlights were no longer shining on him to light him up. It was just completely unexplainable. I never thought of it as a glow, but he seemed somehow illuminated in the dark as I passed because it was so dark out. I still wonder at how I saw him so clearly. It really messed with my head all the way home, and I think about it every time I go by there, even now.

The Presence at Wood Cottage

Around 1988 I was looking to rent a house very cheaply. I saw a very old keeper's cottage for £100/month. Its name was Wood Cottage, and it was ½ mile off a single-track road; no neighbours, no electricity, water pumped up twice a day and gas lighting.

Judging by the layout and bricks, it was much older than it first appeared, and I think it was originally a pair of cottages.

Once I'd settled in, I was keenly aware that there was 'something' around the bathroom/back door area. Not a particularly malevolent thing, but equally, I didn't wish to irritate it.

I recall one still Saturday afternoon, I was cleaning my 2CV. All the doors were ajar on the motor, and I stepped away to enjoy a cigarette.

I turned back to the car, only to see all four doors slowly open.

I shouted, 'Will you stop *that*. You know it scares me ****less.'

All four doors slowly closed, and I said 'Thank *you*.'

The only heating was an open fire. On one occasion, a friend visited, and we were sitting on the settee in the beamed living room, with the fire blazing away. Suddenly, the temperature dropped very swiftly indeed. I did everything I could to encourage the fire, but with no joy. Eventually, the room became warm once more, but we were both very uneasy afterwards.

In time, I moved into a caravan elsewhere. A friend came over to visit and said, 'This is SO pleasant compared to Wood Cottage - I always felt uneasy around the back door and the stables, there was definitely something around that area . . .'

I hadn't mentioned anything to her when she visited, as I didn't want her to be alarmed, BUT, we'd both picked up the same sensations.

The cottage is still there, but unoccupied. The trees I planted have grown over the past thirty-odd years, and it's almost become one with the wood nearby.

When I visited four years ago, I was more than happy to leave, as I think it was still 'occupied' by the same somewhat oppressive feeling.

The dwelling was open, and I ventured in, but my fearless Jack Russell declined to follow.

Who is this that Turns the Pages?

After leaving School I went straight into a job at the Oxford University Press, Walton Street, Oxford. I was part of the typing pool. We were all coached and guided by an elderly lady whose name escapes me, but she was kind of like our guardian, and the go-to if we had problems. One day she said she was planning a tour for us of the top-level rooms of this very old building. She further said that the top level, which was quite huge, held a copy of every book ever printed at the Press. So, we went in groups of about ten people at a time, and were allowed to look at the books but not to handle them. It was fascinating stuff: there was this tiny, tiniest Bible, and in comparison a huge Bible whose pages would need to be turned by two people. We were all happy and making lots of noise, when she called us to stand around her and said, 'I want everyone to be silent, totally silent.' So in that silence we started to hear what sounded like the pages of a book being turned, despite the fact that no one else was up there, and this museum was always locked. But we all heard it. She told us it was a phenomenon that had no explanation; cleaners in the past had heard it, as well as many other people over the years. We left that room feeling very spooked.

An American Airman in Oxford

In 1969, my husband, our three-year-old son and I moved into a council house on the outskirts of Oxford. It was a modern house, and we enjoyed the 18 months we lived there. But in that 18 months our son would quite often come into our bedroom and ask to sleep in our bed. When we asked him why he would say that the man in his room kept waking him up. We'd check the room, but nothing was ever out of place, and we put it down to bad dreams. However, we moved to Devon, and two years later while visiting my parents in Oxford we thought we'd go back to the housing estate and visit friends. We had a lovely afternoon catching up, and our friend casually asked if we'd seen anything strange in the house we lived in. We didn't answer straight off, so he went rummaging in a sideboard and brought out a copy of the *Oxford Mail* and said, 'Read that.' Apparently, after we left a family moved in, and after a short time, fled from the house. They said that in one of the bedrooms family members had seen a man in uniform, just standing there and staring. The newspaper running the story had subsequently done a check on what was there before the housing estate was built, and found that it had been occupied by an American Air base. We were shocked, and then realised that our son's sleepless nights were obviously not bad dreams at all.

A Modern Mystery at Avebury

The following inexplicable occurrence happened in December 1981 or 1982, I forget which. I had hired a large transit van, and together with my husband, our eleven-year-old son, and my brother, we had driven around the south of England delivering pottery to shops who had ordered from us.

On our way back home to Yorkshire we decided to pay a visit to the stone circle at Avebury. The carpark was covered in a thick blanket of pristine snow. We drove straight to the entrance gate, and climbed over as it was closed to visitors. We spent several hours communing with the stones, soaking up the atmosphere and generally relishing the fact that there were no other visitors ruining the ambience by chattering and laughing. When it began to get dark we made our way back to the carpark, and to our horror, the van had gone.

There were tyre tracks in the snow where we had driven in, but none going out, so unless someone could perform the impossible feat of reversing in the exact same tracks without deviating by so much as a centimetre, there was no way the van could have gone. Dismayed and astonished, we began to walk to the carpark entrance. As we came to a right hand bend we saw our van parked in the very furthest corner, but there were no tyre tracks: the snow was absolutely pristine. It had not snowed at all that day, so it couldn't have been driven and then the tracks refilled with snow. We were completely mystified; not quite scared but certainly awestruck. We walked over to the van leaving four sets of footprints and climbed in. We drove out in complete silence. None of us had spoken a word since we first saw that the van was missing. There was just nothing to say. We didn't mention it until we were safely home in Yorkshire.

The Doctor in Black

This story concerns my own house. It is in that sense a 'personal' ghost story, albeit one at second hand, for it was related to me by another villager who used to live in this cottage with his family several decades ago. This is what he told me.

At the time that the alleged occurrences took place he was a child, and slept in the small bedroom to the rear of the house. His bedroom door opened out onto the smallest of landing areas, which was faced by the doors to the two other bedrooms. On a number of nights he recalls that the dwelling was filled with the sound of a wailing infant, but as he and his siblings were well past such an age as to screech in this fashion, it was from no member of the family that these cries issued. He distinctly recalls that he would then hear a tread upon the stairs, and shortly after see a male figure, dressed in a black coat with a wide-brimmed hat of the same colour, pass his open door. It was plain that the figure was making for the bedroom furthest from his own. This is the room from which issued the plaintive cries of the baby, that ceased shortly after the mysterious individual presumably entered the room. After a brief interval, he would see this man in black once more pass his open door, and head back down the stairs. In his hand, he carried a large leather bag. There were no more cries. This same sequence of events is said to have played out on a number of occasions.

It was the opinion of the individual who related this story that the man he had seen was 'a doctor', which might be a reasonable supposition in unreasonable circumstances. If, indeed, this phantom belonged to this particular profession, what was it that he did to still the infant's cries, and why was his shade seemingly doomed to return and repeat this act over and over?

Since we have moved into our 'new' home we have had no such experiences. No man in black has stalked the stairs, and no unfathomable wailing has pierced the night. However, one morning I woke early before daybreak, and as I lay in bed in the darkness pondering the coming day, I heard a series of strange cracks and bangs coming from the kitchen, which is where our short flight of stairs terminates. There was a pause, and then they resumed. Curious as to what the source of these sounds might be, and wondering if a rat had somehow found its way inside and was now playing merry havoc amidst the crockery, I made my way downstairs. The same sounds came intermittently, sharp and distinct. I flicked the light switch. There was nothing out of the ordinary to meet the eye. The cracks and bangs resumed. The gale without was gaining force, and then the cause of this mystery suggested itself. I opened the back door, and sure enough I beheld the cause: acorns. The oaks on the opposite side of the road had produced an abundant crop of acorns that year, and it was these, hitting the door and the roof of our outhouse, that lay at the root of the racket.

We have lately learned that our cottage dates back to the 1670s, for a datestone in the neighbouring property bears the legend of 1676. The house has thus stood long enough to witness many a drama, even in so small a village as this, and as I type, I am sitting in that very room that the ghostly doctor was seen to enter.

Soldiers' Footsteps at Dover Castle

I used to work at Dover Castle. Of the many ghostly sightings it has been famed for, this one took place away from the usual tourist route.

It was Christmas Eve, and I was working alone finishing off a report before going home. My office was in a Victorian barrack block, which was the store for thousands of historical artefacts, from sites all round Kent. These included ancient human remains, so you never quite felt alone.

My desk was on the first floor in a room that had been a long dormitory for soldiers, illuminated by a row of tall windows. It was around three o'clock, so although not yet dark, the sun was low and I sat with the lights on.

When you are used to working in a busy office, concentrating on your work, the sound of the door to the stairs opening and closing, as well as footsteps on the stairs, are things which you hear but tend to ignore. On this occasion, however, I wondered who it might be, but no more than that. I distinctly heard the steps come up to the office door which then opened, but not fully. I turned round to see who it was, only to see that there was no one there, as the door slowly slid back into place. Maybe whoever it was had changed their mind and gone elsewhere? But as I looked in the direction of the door, you can only imagine my surprise as I heard the footsteps sound upon the floor and continue into the room. Then they came to a stop, and something even stranger happened: they started once more, but this time I heard the steps pace up the wall behind me and onto the ceiling. They were *overhead.*

I laughed, and spoke to the air, 'Okay, I get the hint,' and closed down my computer and went home.

The Linguistically Precocious Two-Year-Old

This story still amazes me now, and I often ask myself if it really happened. If I hadn't told others about it on the actual day, I'd still think that I dreamt it.

In 2007, when my daughter was only two, I took her up to Manchester to visit my aunt. She had lived in the same house all her life (and still does) and both my uncle (her husband, Philip) and my grandmother passed away in the main upstairs bedroom. It was my first visit to see her with my daughter, who, being so little, knew nothing of the history and had never met my grandmother or uncle, both of whom died when I was very young.

One afternoon, I took my daughter upstairs to change her nappy. I laid her on the bathroom floor but she was very fractious and kept twisting away from me to look towards the window. When I asked her what was wrong she replied, 'Philip is here,' and pointed to the corner. I immediately sat back and looked around the room but could see no one, although the hairs on my neck and arms were by now standing on end. I asked my daughter where exactly he was, and she pointed to the window and casually said, 'Oh, he's gone to the park now on his bike, but he said to tell you that he loves you, and he loves me too.'

The bike held no significance at all for me, but it seemed an oddly adult thing for a two year old to say and I was really quite shaken. I was conflicted for a little while as to whether to mention this to my aunt, as she was living alone in the house and she missed my uncle dreadfully, even though he had been dead for over 30 years. In the end, I decided she would probably like to know. She's a very no nonsense, sensible kind of lady, and I felt a bit embarrassed telling her, but she immediately smiled and told me that she knew he was there, and had felt his presence many times, although she'd never seen anything herself. To this day, my daughter doesn't remember a thing about it and always laughs at me when I tell the story.

The Apple Tree Guardian

There used to be an orchard growing in the back garden of the house that I grew up in. Before I was born, the orchard was cut down but one apple tree remained. I used to climb that tree a lot during my childhood.

It's a well-known story in my family that one day when I was about four I came in from the garden and said to my mother, "Mum, Papa came and warned me. He said, 'Beware Jonathan, get down from the tree!'"

My mother thought this was quite unusual, partly in that I wouldn't have been using the word 'beware' at that age, but mainly because 'Papa' is how my family referred to my grandfather who had died a year before I was born.

A few weeks after this my aunt was on a train with a friend of the family's, and the friend asked, 'How are the children?' meaning my sister and I.

My aunt proceeded to tell her this story about me coming in from the garden and weirdly telling my mother about my grandfather's warning. Immediately, the woman went all ashen faced, and my aunt asked her, 'What's the matter with you?' The lady reminded my aunt that her uncle, Papa's brother, had fallen out of an apple tree at a young age. A wound on his leg had become gangrenous and he had died as a result. Because of this story I have always seen my grandfather as a guardian angel or protector.

The Paddington Ghost

As a child I had a few ghostly and spiritual experiences, but the one that scared me happened as an adult thirty-odd years ago. I travelled to Sydney alone for a holiday, as I had a few friends living there and I was trying to decide whether to emigrate. I planned my month well in advance, but one friend - Sarah - left to live in New Zealand, and she was letting her home in Paddington to another friend called Maggie. Maggie kindly said I could stay but would have to sleep on a mattress on the large upstairs landing as she had another friend staying in the spare bedroom. I didn't care, and accepted as I was only going to stay a few nights.

That first night, I awoke on my back bathed in a cold sweat, gripped by a sense of terror as someone, or some *thing*, was squeezing with their hands up from my ankles to my knees. I screamed and flailed out with my hands, but there was nothing there. I knew Maggie didn't have any pets, and it felt like hands, not paws. No one came out of their rooms, and I questioned Maggie who seemed uncomfortable and denied hearing me scream.

The second night I was awoken with a hard shove as something pushed my right shoulder (again I was on my back), and by a woman's whispering in my right ear. Again I was terrified, but could not understand what she was saying. By then I'd had enough, as the whole of the upstairs of that house in Paddington gave me the creeps, so I left after that second night. Maggie contacted me a few months later to say she too had felt something watching her, but hadn't wanted to tell me at the time.

She asked the neighbours who used to live there before my friend Sarah, and was told the story about a young woman who had committed suicide by hanging herself from the ceiling lamp on the top landing – which happened to have been the one hanging directly above the mattress I had been sleeping on. After hearing this explanation, Maggie asked a priest to come and give an exorcism to help the unhappy spirit leave the house. What, if anything, happened after this, I do not know.

The Bobbed Photographer of Speke Hall

I would like to share with you an incident that happened three years ago,[4] while visiting Speke Hall on the outskirts of Liverpool.

My fiancée and I decided we would visit the hall on a Sunday afternoon in the summer. The weather was lovely, very sunny and warm.

We parked up on the grass car park in the grounds of the hall, and made our way to the admission booth. Next to this is a coffee shop, and being a lover of coffee, I bought myself one. We took our drinks and sat at a table, which overlooked the small bridge which leads to the entrance of the hall (if you haven't been there, it's well worth a visit if you should be in the area).

We sat and looked at the beautiful trees and flowers, watching the visitors, of whom there were quite a few, walking to and from the house. It was then that I noticed a young lady on the bridge, probably in her late twenties, with what looked like an old box camera. She had a bob

---

[4] Three years before the first Covid lockdown, so 2017.

style hairdo, and was dressed in a pair of cream-coloured trousers and a high-neck blouse. She seemed to be looking at the other visitors, watching them and observing the photographic equipment that they had. It almost seemed as if she felt that their cameras were of an inferior quality to the one which she owned. She just stood there, on the bridge, while I drank my coffee. I mentioned her to my fiancée, but to my surprise, she said she could see no one of that description. To me, however, her image was as clear as day.

Once I had finished my coffee, we made our way into the house. It is a splendid house, with lots to see in its many rooms, filled with historic furniture, ornaments and curios. It took some time for us to get around the property, but all the time we were there I was thinking of the young lady on the bridge.

When we came to the end of our tour we went to the souvenir shop. Towards the back of the shop was a room filled with second-hand books for sale. Being an avid reader, I wanted to go in to see what was available. I was soon engrossed, and after leafing through numerous books was called over to a table by my fiancée on which a collection of old cameras was displayed. To my surprise, there were four pictures of the very lady that I had described on the bridge. What was even more surprising, however, was the revelation that she had lived at the house in the 1920s. She had been an avid photographer, and also enjoyed flying. A short history of her life was displayed in the room where the books were being sold.

Although hard to believe, I'm convinced I saw her on the bridge. I consider myself fortunate to have seen her in vivid colour, as opposed to the black and white pictures displayed in the small library. I shall visit again, just to see if I can catch a glimpse of this lady once more.

Baby Boy in January

The hospital I trained at in the early 1980s was one of those really old ones, parts of which used to be the local workhouse. Long before care in the community was a thing, there were a lot of poor old souls who had been abandoned in the 'asylum' wards by their families who just couldn't cope with them because there was no support. Then there were those who had had no business being there in the first place, but had been there so long that they were completely institutionalised and would have been incapable of living independently. Indeed, many of them had become more disturbed due to their early incarceration rather than being admitted because of any particular mental infirmity.

One such lady was 'Rose'. She was about 80. She used to wander the corridors carrying a doll which she talked and sang to. She was amiable and easy-going, and had the manner of a compliant, eager-to-please child. I discovered that she had originally been admitted to the asylum as a teenager for being 'wilful and morally degenerate.' From the notes of the time, it appeared that she had been admitted due to becoming pregnant (I don't know the circumstances), which had scandalised her family, and so they had sent her to the asylum. I have no idea what happened to the baby. It may even be possible that Rose had a learning difficulty and we often wondered if she had been abused within the family.

Anyway, Rose was helping me to set the tables in the dining room. She had put her doll, which she called Lizzie, in a chair, wrapped in a blanket. My colleague, who was trying for a baby, was with us. Rose looked at her and said, unusually clearly, 'Baby Boy in January. How lovely!' My colleague said, 'Rose, how do you know?' Rose looked at her doll and said, 'Lizzie told me.'

This happened at Easter, so if my colleague was pregnant, it was really recent. Yes. My colleague did have a baby boy on January 3rd the following year.

Two Cribs

A tale told by my grandfather, a no-nonsense man who certainly didn't believe in ghosts. We are talking 1947, not so long after the war, and at that time his wife – my grandmother – had just given birth to twins. To make sure that they could always keep an eye on them, the two cribs were placed at the foot of their bed.

My grandfather told me that he woke to see a shadowy figure standing over one of the cribs. He sat up in bed there for a moment, gathering his senses, and perhaps not quite believing what he saw, tried to shake my grandmother awake. She didn't wake quickly, but once she had woken she didn't see anything, and whereas for my grandfather the vision had only lasted a few seconds, it felt like a lifetime. They both leapt out of bed to see if the twins were okay, and sadly one of them, baby John, was found to be blue and lifeless. My grandfather said he just knew before he had even looked at the baby that he was gone. The child was a victim of cot death, and my grandfather believes that the Spirit of Death visited their house that night to collect their baby.

I have goosebumps as I am typing this.

My grandfather was so matter-of-fact about the vision. Of course, my grandparents were devastated about losing their baby, but it was just after the war, and people were trying to make the best of things and he kept himself busy earning money to feed his large family. He never spoke of this story, and the death of his baby son, unless pushed to do so.

'What are you doing in my house?'

Our current house is a lovely old granite pile, not far from the sea. There is literally nothing spooky about it, despite its period details. Except for on this one occasion.

My husband was dozing in a chair downstairs. As he woke from his snooze an aged woman in slippers and dressing gown suddenly came bustling out of the kitchen. She was completely bald, and clearly hadn't expected to be seeing anyone. She started when she saw my husband sitting there, as if to say: 'Who are you and what are you doing in my house?'

But as she looked, her eyes glazed over, and then it was as if she couldn't see him any more. The woman blinked a few times, then carried on her way, walking laboriously out of the room and up the stairs, disappearing from sight.

'You're dreaming,' my husband told himself.

That evening, when I got home from work, he told me of the woman he'd seen, but for some reason we didn't think much of it really, dismissing it as just a dream. Now, we live in the west of Cornwall and to be honest it's quite a small community. Some weeks later, when my husband was speaking to a colleague at work, the conversation turned to where each of them lived, and when his colleague heard that we lived on such-and-such street their ears pricked up.

'Oh really,' they said, 'my old nan used to live on that street. She got cancer and lost her hair and everything. She died there in the end, poor thing. So what number do you guys live at?'

Unsurprisingly, it was our house.

Back on the Market

Just a little story from about twenty-five years ago. Where we lived we became very friendly with an elderly neighbour called Margaret who lived across the road from us. Margaret was divorced and lived there on her own as her two children had both gone to live abroad.

She was a keen gardener and could often be seen tending her front garden which was a riot of colour. Her house was in a very elevated position which gave passers-by a good view of her lovely garden and lots of people would stop for a chat. We talked most days on my way to and from school, taking and collecting my children.

Sadly, she became ill with cancer. I visited her in hospital, and she asked how her garden was looking. I told her the daffs were all in bloom and it looked lovely. 'I hope whoever buys my house will care for the garden,' she said.

After she died, and about six months later, the house had been sold and I was driving past and noticed the new lady owner mowing the grass. Smiling to myself thinking Margaret will be pleased, I looked again and waved to . . . Margaret, who was standing in the window watching. Ten full seconds elapsed before the full shock hit me as to what I had just seen — Margaret was dead, so how could it be her?

Some months later the house was back on the market. The lady who had bought the house told me, 'I am not happy here; some odd things have been happening: items moved about, things going missing and lights constantly being turned on and off.'

I thought it best to say nothing about seeing Margaret, whom I had watched cutting her grass six months previously. I have never forgotten this experience, and can still picture Margaret so clearly dressed in her habitual orange sweatshirt. We moved ourselves not long after, so I do not know if the new owners have had any odd things happening in Margaret's old home.

A 'slim and girlish physique'

A contemporary ghost story, this happened to me three Christmases ago.[5]

Ruminating on my tasks for the day I somewhat wistfully peered out of the bus window, observing pedestrians encumbered with bulging shopping bags, hurriedly heading home to peel parsnips, roast chestnuts and wrap last minute treasures in gaudy paper before safely ensconcing them beneath their Christmas trees.

I sighed at the thought of the labour ahead of me, for although it was only shopping, I envied those who were done with such undertakings.

Taking in the sights of festively decorated windows, behind which stood proud conifers adorned with multi-coloured baubles and vibrant fairy lights, I longed to be finished for the day; spending done, food refrigerated, gifts swathed in tissue and ribbons.

The bus slowed to a stop to allow more passengers to alight and my attention was suddenly caught by a familiar figure: inside a tanning salon I spied Stacey, an old friend from my youth. I marvelled to myself about how fantastic she looked: her coal black hair expertly coiffured into upswept spikes, her still slim and girlish physique encased in leather and lace and a stack of silver bangles glistening on both of her bone-white, slender wrists.

Back in the day we had both competed to be the queen of the Goth scene, and although on that particular day Stacey would have won hands down, I couldn't help

---

[5] This would have been the Christmas of 2018.

but giggle to myself – a Goth with a tan? What was she thinking? No self-respecting Goth would be seen dead in a tanning salon, surely?

Continuing on my journey, I couldn't help but muse on the sighting of my friend. The years hadn't treated me too badly, but she had looked a total knockout; she didn't seem to have aged at all.

Later that evening, my chores complete, I mentioned the encounter to my fiancé. He laughingly suggested she had discovered the elixir of youth and I had to agree with him. In a subsequent phone call to a mutual friend I discussed the experience at some length bemoaning the fact of the passing years as together we pondered what Stacey's secret could possibly be. Just as I was intending to retire for the night my phone beeped shrilly, indicating a late-night text from my aforementioned pal. Rather ominously the message read 'Check Facebook.'

Thinking she could only be referring to our earlier conversation, I logged in and tentatively typed Stacey's full name into the search bar. Upon reaching her page I read the most current post and my blood ran cold . . . it was a heartfelt message from her beloved husband, lamenting the sad passage of his beautiful wife who had been cruelly taken from him by cancer. It seemed she had been ill for some time, and had lost her battle with the dreadful disease only the day before.

As I brooded on this tragic state of affairs, experiencing the bitter sweet remembrance of our friendship and epic nights out together, an unexpected recollection hit me like a bolt from the blue: Sundaze

Tanning Salon had previously been an insurance brokers with a cosy flat above; a flat where Stacey and her then boyfriend Michael had resided for a time; a place where we had all shared some fabulous times and made some very wonderful memories.

Up the Garden Path

My friend and her husband bought a very old run down cottage in Essex many years ago. It had been empty for quite some time and needed a lot of work, but it was set in a very large garden with lovely views, and they could see the potential to make it a lovely home.

The day they moved in it was chaos with removal men, boxes and furniture everywhere. There were about eight people in the house and it was all a bit cramped, so my friend decided she would risk the ladder and go and make a start on making up a bed. I must explain that the stairs were considered dangerous owing to their wood being rotten so a ladder had been brought in to serve in its stead.

She found the sheets and started making the bed. As she shook the quilt cover she looked out of the window to see an old lady walking up the long and narrow garden path carrying a basket up towards the house. *Oh, how nice!* She thought a neighbour was calling to say hello and to welcome them. So she quickly finished putting the quilt on the bed, and gingerly made her way back down the ladder hoping to speak to her; it only took a minute or two.

Everyone was still milling about opening boxes and positioning furniture. My friend asked if the old lady had knocked, but the others all looked perplexed: 'What old lady?' No one had knocked. Even so, she went out and looked all around for the old lady, but the unexpected caller was nowhere to be seen.

This really puzzled my friend because she had clearly seen the old woman walking up the garden path and could describe her clothes, the basket she was carrying and several other details concerning her appearance.

Some weeks later she found herself chatting to a local shop keeper and happened to ask about the previous owners of the old cottage. The shopkeeper said it was an old lady who had lived there all her life; she had never married and had a routine of visiting the village shops every day to do her tiny bit of shopping and loved to chat to everyone she met. The cottage fell into disrepair over the years, he said, and when she died it was another year before the house was put on the market. 'Hold on,' he said, 'I have a picture of her taken at a village fete,' and yes — you've guessed it.

The old lady she had seen walking up the garden path carrying the basket was *her*. She was even holding the selfsame basket in the picture. My friend and her husband loved that old cottage and completely renovated it, staying there for over ten years. They never saw the old lady again, but my friend always said she had to come to visit the new owners and check them out.

The Birtley Cellar

Some years ago I had a second job as a barmaid in an old pub in Birtley, County Durham, which was haunted by a previous landlady. This lady had committed suicide by gassing herself in the pub kitchen. After death, she would frequently turn the gas off to the beer pumps in the cellar. I personally never saw her, but the landlady and landlord had seen her several times. The landlord was a musician and had a studio in the cellar (brave chap), but he and his wife got so used to her that they just talked to her. If we had a lot of customers and she turned off the gas, the landlady would go to the cellar, turn it back on, and ask her to please leave it alone as the pub was busy. This pub was a listed building and has now been converted into an old people's home, and I often wonder if she is still there, and if she turns their gas off.

Snooker Spirit

As a child in Bath I saw spirits from time to time, and was sometimes scared, sometimes just curious. A particular incident really threw me into a panic, though, and I remember all the details vividly to this day, with one exception - the name of the building where it took place.

I lived on Cedric Road in Weston Village and when I was about nine years old a friend and I used to sneak across to an old building on Combe Park. We were a little wild and often played in the Royal United Hospital grounds, especially around the boiler house, where we would annoy the staff hugely. The door to this ancient house was often unlocked, so we used to creep in and then play snooker. It seemed to be empty, so I suspect it had some community use in the evenings as there was a hall nearby used by scouts and other worthy groups.

The building was strange and darkly exciting to us. It was called something like The Priory or Hermitage or Grange, but I can't remember, annoyingly, and it has since been demolished. Anyway, apparently it was home to priests in the past, and still had the air of a church-like silent mustiness.

One day we entered on tiptoe as usual, found the place empty and set up the balls ready to play. It was a beautiful old snooker table and we were both keen players even at that age. No sooner had we set everything up than we heard footsteps coming along the old panelled corridor. It had bare floorboards which creaked as well as amplifying the noise of the footsteps themselves; only this time there was no creaking, just loud echoing footsteps, as if the person had placed no weight on the boards but was walking on a flagstone floor.

Of course we were in a panic and tried to hide, but the room was sparsely furnished so our only hope was to cower under the snooker table itself. This proved to be our biggest mistake.

The footsteps paused, and then resumed, moving across the floor towards us. But there were no legs to be seen, no movement at all, just the sound of the spirit walking - for we knew by then this must be a ghost. Still we hid, shaking and exchanging terrified glances, not wanting to move in case we were grabbed.

The atmosphere grew menacing, and it felt to us as though this entity really didn't want us there. A short click reached our ears, as if someone was touching the snooker balls, then a cacophony of clattering accelerated and amplified, vibrating and shaking us to our core as all the balls on the table were being swept about so violently that some flew from the table across the floor.

We'd had enough. We exchanged a glance of terror and threw ourselves towards the door. The latch would not move, not an inch (I know this is a movie cliché, but that is how it was). There was a cackle, or so we believed, and then the door released and we hurtled out into the fresh air, not stopping our flight until we were across the main road and almost home.

I'd like to say that we never returned, but one evening, after sufficient time had passed for us to recover from our ordeal, we did, partly out of bravado and partly out of curiosity. As I say, we were a little wild. One of the scouting groups was using the hall nearby and we hit on the idea of performing our own 'haunting'. We grabbed a couple of snooker balls each and crept through the side door of the hall.

Kneeling down we rolled the balls across the wooden stage floor, making ghostly whistles and whoops as we did so. The kids were satisfyingly terrified and we ran out cackling to ourselves as young boys do, only to find ourselves pursued by three adults, each looking vaguely ridiculous in their shorts. We ran up some steps to the roof of the hall and hid, to no avail. In those days justice was swift and after some tearful bruising we shuffled across the roof towards the stairs, humiliated and regretful, but still a little pleased with our adventure.

From the corner of my eye I swear there was the shadow of a cassocked figure, nodding sagely.

A Headless Rabbit

This happened in 2006. My husband's nana died, and for weeks after he would have 3 a.m. conversations with her. I would normally sleep through them, but then he would wake up drained and upset and then I would be awake too. I sometimes caught the end of the conversation and my husband's end was perfectly clear. To explain, if my husband talks in his sleep it's always a load of nonsense and slurred. This wasn't, it was a clear conversation. Anyway, it all came to a head one night when I woke up at the start and heard the whole thing. Now I was terrified (not sure why, I loved his nana). The conversation covered a lot of stuff including one of our cats: 'Our cat? Poppy? The black one? Oh yeah she's a killer, brings in all sorts.' Then it turned creepy: 'You're going? Why? Oh, Karen's awake and she's a bit scared; okay then. I'll speak to you again. Bye.'

He then woke up exhausted, surprised to see me starting at him in horror. I told him I'd heard the whole chat and what was said. He was quite upset and filled in the bits (his nana) that I couldn't hear including what she said about our cat always killing wildlife. And then he went to the loo (like he always did after these episodes) and let out the biggest girly scream. The reason was that there was a headless rabbit in the bathroom.

Anyway, after that incident things calmed down. He only had the nana visits every couple of months until his dad died, and then he would have nightly conversations with him. There have been other things that happen to my husband, but . . .

The Gamekeeper

Back in the summer of 2005 I was given a job to paint the inside of an empty house on a large country estate. On arrival we had a look around, then began work upstairs, and being so warm we held the downstairs doors open with full five-litre cans of paint to try to encourage any breeze to blow through the house.

After lunch we both went to the separate rooms where we were working and started again. I couldn't tell you how long it was until a door downstairs slammed shut with such force that I dropped the brush I was holding. On walking across the landing to the stairs I passed my colleague who was still working.

Downstairs I found the full paint can had been moved as if the door had slid it across the floor to slam shut, so I put it back as it was and went back upstairs. No sooner had I got back upstairs than BANG! The door had slammed shut again. Four times this happened, and on the fourth time of opening the door I looked to my right through the kitchen into the dining room and saw a figure of a man dressed in green wearing a flat cap move into the living room, so I gave chase. As I entered the empty room I was met with a freezing chill in the air that made every hair on my head stand on end. I questioned myself for a while, but I know what I saw that day.

A few days later I met the estate's maintenance man and mentioned my experience. His reply, delivered in an old Oxfordshire accent, was 'Ah boy, that be the old gamekeeper. He were killed on the road there. That were his place.' Turns out I wasn't the first to meet the keeper since his passing.

On the Road to Nowhere

The weekly grocery shop seldom provides the stuff of which lasting memories are made, for I do not tend to find myself reflecting upon the 'thrill' of happening upon unanticipated two-for-one deals, or a 3p reduction in the cost of a head of celery. Supermarket supremos may wish that it were otherwise, but that's just how it is.

One recent Saturday morning, however, will not be one that I forget in a hurry, for something most peculiar occurred, and I must admit that I remain quite stumped as to a plausible explanation. My wife and I live in Cumbria, some miles from the nearest town, and had left home a little after eight to purchase the weekly necessities. It was light and overcast; rain was falling and the roads were sheened with water; and the run-off from a neighbouring field had flooded a stretch of the carriageway, providing a moment of doubt as to whether the car would make it through. It did. It was, in other words, a perfectly typical Saturday.

As we headed out past the last of the scattered houses that lie at the edge of the village, we came to a stretch of road leading up to a bend. Beyond it the carriageway may be glimpsed above the hedgerows owing to a prominent rise, and cresting this I saw a silver car travelling towards us at forty or fifty miles per hour. The road is not particularly wide, so I drew closer to the verge and moderated my speed as I went into the corner, aware that we would be meeting the other vehicle within the next two to three seconds. And yet . . . this is where things get strange. As we came round the bend and continued onwards, there was to my surprise, no car to be seen. On we went, up and over the rise, to find the road quite empty. It was at this point that I said to my wife 'Did you see—' and before I had time to complete my sentence she answered, 'That car? Yes, I did.'

'But, it's gone.'

'I know.'

In those two to three seconds that other car had simply disappeared. On that stretch of road you will find no junctions, no lay-bys and no driveways. The missing car had not careered through the hedge and into a neighbouring field, so where could it have gone? There was certainly no time for it to have executed a three-point turn and sped off in the opposite direction. What had happened to it? We remain perplexed.

The Shaking Door

For a couple of months after moving into our house we would hear footsteps on the stairs. Once we heard a bottle falling from the back of the kitchen bench to the floor, but for me the strangest thing that happened took place one morning when I was washing dishes. The sink is next to the back door to the enclosed yard/garden, and has a large window above it. The door is glazed down to waist height, so you can see clearly into the yard through both. At the time, the back door was shut, and our two dogs were sat in the yard a few feet beyond it.

Suddenly, the door started shaking violently and noisily in its frame as though someone had hold of the handle and was shaking it back and forth with great rapidity. I stood looking at it perplexed, a couple of feet away, whereas the dogs stayed where they were on the other side looking right at the noisy door and barking like mad. It wasn't me doing it, and it wasn't them. Remember, I had perfect visibility of the door and the yard through the glass, and there was nobody else there.

A week or so later, I had gone out on a Sunday morning whilst my wife was in bed and the dogs were in the room with her. She heard footsteps coming up the stairs to the closed door. The dogs just sat up and stared with their ears pricked up.

This was the end of the strangeness. My wife put it down to whoever it was having realised that they had scared her, so they stopped.

The Shotwick Ghost

Back in 1995 I was doing some archaeological work around Shotwick in Cheshire, in advance of a new by-pass on the A494 at the junction with the A550. This was mainly looking at the northwestern side of the former Shotwick Deer Park boundary which ran parallel to the A494 at this point. The deer park was part of the royal manor of Castle Shotwick and was enclosed in 1327 by the Justiciar of Chester; the boundary itself originally comprised a ditch, timber palings and a deer leap. Both Shotwick Castle and the nearby village of Shotwick had originally been on the edge of the River Dee, on the English side, prior to it silting up.

The A550/A494 is known locally as Welsh Road and it cuts across the eastern corner of the deer park running north to Two Mills on the Parkgate Road and south over the River Dee in to Flintshire (Wales). This road passes through a dip formed by the Shotwick Brook, wooded on either side, where a crossroads is found with Shotwick Lane. At the time I was working there a story was circulating about a strange phenomenon. On a number of occasions a man had been seen by passing motorists running across Welsh Road in the dip near the crossroads, and had been the cause of a number of minor accidents when people swerved to avoid him. The unknown man had been described by more than one witness as looking over his shoulder whilst running, as though he was being chased by someone. He seemed oblivious to the traffic on the road.

About twelve months later I was doing a daily run out to a site in Cheshire from Mold (Flintshire) in a hire van, which took me along the A494 through Shotwick Deer Park. The road doglegged from north to east as you entered the old deer park, and there were traffic lights on the bend which more often than not changed to red as you reached them. I had a younger member of staff with me, and we had previously discussed ghosts and 'things that go bump in the night'. He was a firm non-believer and had chastised me on more than one occasion for even entertaining the possibility that the supernatural might exist.

On one particular morning, as we pulled away from the lights and I was accelerating around the bend, he suddenly slapped his hands on the dashboard and shouted, 'Jesus, look out!' I immediately took my foot off the accelerator but didn't slam on the breaks as I couldn't see the hazard he was referring too. When I said to him 'What happened?' he replied, 'Didn't you see that bloke running across the road? I can't believe no one hit him!'

The thing was, I hadn't seen anyone run across the road. It was a dual carriageway with a central reservation, with both sides of the road being flanked by dense high hawthorn hedges (the kind not easily forced through or jumped over). Looking in the rear-view mirrors I couldn't see anyone. I questioned my colleague about where the man was, and he went a bit sheepish: 'I don't know; maybe he ran off in to the fields?' 'No chance!' I said. 'Those hedges are too high to get over. I think you've seen the Shotwick ghost!' He wouldn't have it of course: 'There's no such things as ghosts!' However, he couldn't explain what he'd seen, and wouldn't be drawn when I asked him for a more detailed description of what the man was wearing or how he had appeared.

I've always wondered why he saw something and I didn't. After all, I was the driver and more 'open' to seeing something, whereas he could have been taking a kip or reading a book. My eyes were on the road, and yet I saw nothing out of the ordinary whatsoever.

John

I used to live in a lovely seventeenth-century workman's cottage; a beautiful beamed cottage with a large fireplace, original oak flooring, and not a single straight wall or floor. It used to be owned by the Earls of Warwick, and housed the Castle groundsman. I'd not long moved in, and with pride announced I'd host the next Guiders meeting (I was a Brownie leader). I had felt for some time that there was 'something', especially on the stairs, but decided to try and ignore it because of the age of the house. When I first told mum, within the first days of moving in, she said be careful on those stairs; always put the light on.

There had been one or two things we couldn't put our finger on, but this particular night, the night I was hosting, it was almost like *it* decided to show off. Having settled into the meeting, I forgot everything except what we all needed to discuss and arrange. When the time came to close the meeting and we started to talk about the house – its age, its possible past inhabitants – almost right on cue creaks started up above us in my bedroom, and clear as anything, footsteps could be heard pacing across the floor. We all looked at each other as the footsteps creaked across the middle of the floor. Mum said it was my cat, but I pointed at the cat lying curled up in the chair by the downstairs fire. We carried on listening, all sort of accepting what we were hearing (we were all sensitive to that sort of thing; all sorts happened at our Brownie meetings, and other places we visited. It was great.), but I pointed out that although we could hear it crossing the middle of my bedroom floor, whatever it was, was walking right through my bed. At that point, my guests swiftly left.

There were many incidents in that house, with lots of things happening usually when there was a change in energy; when my then boyfriend attacked me and left; then my now hubby moved in, and his very young son; or when my grandad died, and then my mum. Usually you 'felt' something on the stairs, and you sensed that you were being watched. I named him 'John'.

After our little girl was born, there was again another shift in energy. She started walking, and suddenly became frightened of the stairs. She would not go up them on her own. We'd always try and brush it off, make light of it, make a play. Then she said she didn't want to go up the stairs past 'the man'. She said he was lying on the stairs, and he wouldn't let her past. We'd pick her up, and feel the energy on the stairs, knowing we had to do something.

The next night we told her she had to ask him to let her past. She asked him, saying the words which we had told her to use, and she was suddenly able to go up the stairs. I sat on the stairs afterwards, and told him he wasn't allowed to frighten our little girl anymore. We were happy for him to be there; he belongs there, after all, but we weren't happy for him to frighten her. After that, there were no more issues.

I felt so sad leaving that house. I walk past it quite regularly, and wonder who has it now, and whether 'John' is happy with his new lodgers.

The Girl in the Brown Dress

About thirty-five years ago[6] my husband, myself and our two young daughters went on holiday to Torquay. We stayed in a flat in an old house; sadly, I can't remember whereabouts it was, but it looked like an Italianate style villa with a small tower. Our daughters had a bedroom along from ours up a few steps. On the first night I woke up to find a small girl standing by my bed. I just thought it was one of my daughters, and said, 'What's the matter? Can't you sleep?' Suddenly though, I realised it wasn't either of my girls, as she had wavy hair and was wearing a brown dress with a white pinafore over it; she had tears running down her face, and seemed to be rubbing her hands together. I turned over to my husband and woke him up, but when I turned back the little girl had gone. My husband said I was dreaming, and went straight back

---

[6] Towards the end of the 1980s.

to sleep. I didn't find the experience frightening, but didn't sleep much the rest of that night.

In the morning my youngest daughter came down crying as the fluffy toy rabbit she usually took to bed was missing. We searched the bedroom and couldn't find it until we discovered one of the beds had a drawer in the base. We pulled it out, and the rabbit was at the back of the drawer. My younger daughter was by now angry and accused her sister of hiding her toy. This, however, was impossible, as the drawer was very difficult to open. I did wonder if the little ghost girl had hidden the rabbit to play with later. The rest of the holiday passed without incident. I never saw the girl again, and the rabbit stayed in bed with my daughter. In a way I was disappointed, as I'd have liked to see the little girl again, as I'd have liked to ask her why she was so upset.

A Long Island Ghost Story

I lived on Long Island, Suffolk County, and seventy-five miles out from Manhattan. My grandmother lived with her son, my uncle, in Queens, a suburb of the city. My cousin Edna lived with her father in Queens, Elmhurst, to be exact.

I was to spend the summer in Queens at my cousin's house. I don't remember how long into that summer this happened. The house was old, probably dating from the late 1800s. It had a basement that felt haunted, and it had three bedrooms on the upstairs, and a main floor only a few steps up from the street. My cousin Edna's was the one in the middle, with all of the bedrooms being located on the same side of the house. Her bedroom, rectangular in shape and narrow, was right off the kitchen, and my uncle always kept a little nightlight on in the kitchen that lit the entrance to her room, creating a long pale area of light that stretched right into it; the door to her room was never shut. My Uncle was a night worker and not home at the time; it was late – around midnight.

We had gone to bed, but being about eleven and twelve were lying talking in the dark in bed. The head of the bed was at the opposite end of the narrow side of the rectangle. Straight ahead of us to the left was the open doorway to the kitchen, with that shaft of light stretching across the wooden floor.

My cousin was loud when she spoke; she never could speak quietly. I, on the other hand, spoke nearly in a whisper so as not to get into trouble with my grandma, who was sleeping in the bedroom that was on the other side of the wall behind us. We were, after all, supposed to be asleep.

Suddenly, my cousin said, in her usual loud voice, 'Who is THAT? Who IS THAT LADY?' and I looked at the doorway and saw standing in it an old woman. Her hair was black with streaks of gray and pulled back in a bun, and she wore a long black skirt that went all the way down to the floor, and a white, long-sleeved blouse. She wore a stern look on her face, and stared straight ahead, not toward us, as if she was not aware of us (we were to her right). It was NOT my grandmother. I was terrified. I had never seen this woman before in my life, and there was not supposed to be anyone in the house but us and our grandmother. Honestly, I remember wishing my cousin would be quiet. I was so afraid, and I did not want this woman to hear her and see us. She stood in the doorway a few minutes, staring into space with that fixed stern stare.

And then, to our horror, this woman began to move forward across the front of the room in that shaft of light; not walking though, more like floating. Her skirt never changed position as if she were walking; she never moved her legs, but drifted silently, slowly, and then made the turn into the direction of my side of the bed, coming straight down toward me. My side of the bed had about three feet to the outside wall; it was only a narrow pathway. She was going to come to within inches from me.

At my side of the head of the bed, behind me, was a closet; one without a door, just an old gray cloth hanging from a rod covering the opening. When she came down the side of the bed toward me I became so frightened I closed my eyes and froze. I opened them and took a peek just seconds after closing them, and slightly turned my head to follow her as she passed right by me, only to see her 'float through' that hanging cloth, seemingly completely unaware of us. The cloth had not parted, she just floated on through it like it wasn't there and into the closet.

I think we talked about it in bed right after she disappeared, but I do not remember. I can't imagine why we did not jump up out of the bed and leave the room, but what we did next, I cannot recall.

The Syston Procession

The following incident occurred sometime in the mid-seventies. Living in Syston at that time, I used to frequent Leicester city centre for nights out. At weekends I would often get a lift home from a friend, who would drop me off (at my request) on the forecourt of a filling station. From there I would cross the main road, the A607, and walk home up the avenue opposite.

On one particular night, around 2.20 a.m., I was dropped off as usual, crossed the road and walked up the avenue, not thinking about anything much and looking forward to some sleep. I hadn't walked very far when I heard music coming from the main road. It sounded as if it was approaching from the direction of Melton Mowbray to the north, so I stopped and stood looking at the end of the avenue, expecting to see the source of the sounds, for the music appeared to be getting closer. I waited a while, but nothing came into view, so, out of curiosity, I walked back to the main road and looked north. I was fully expecting the source of the mysterious music be revealed; I didn't expect the road to be empty, but there was no traffic, and no other people about. And yet the music still sounded as if it were only a few metres away, heading slowly southwards towards where I was standing. My immediate thought was that it had to be from someone's hi-fi, probably because the windows had been left open, but I soon realised the sound was too three dimensional and pervasive, just as live musicians would sound outdoors.

It's not easy to describe the music, but this is my impression: there was a slow drumbeat, about one beat every two seconds; it was a low boom rather that a sharp drum sound, overlaid with several wind instruments. I imagined something like a bamboo flute with a breathy tone which was mid-pitch, not high and trilling, and over this was a chorus of voices, sounding like male and female vocals harmonising, with the female voices predominant. They were singing, or chanting; this was a fluid, floating melody, gentle and slightly subdued. It was nothing resembling plain chant or any folk music I had previously heard; to my ears it sounded more pagan than anything else. It progressed along the middle of the road as if with solemn purpose, neither joyful nor gloomy, but somehow purposeful.

More curious now, I walked north along the main road on the right-hand side, towards the 'procession', which still sounded as if it was coming closer, but as I walked, it receded back along the road, all the while still sounding as if it was coming towards me. As I continued walking, I looked to my left and right, looking for lights on in the row of 1930s semis on my right, and a few recently-built homes to my left. I could see no lights in any building and no windows open, which was not surprising as it was a chilly and damp February night. I also listened hard in case I could detect the origin of the sounds. In the event, I thought that I was hearing a very late rehearsal for some outdoor event, or a very good and powerful hi-fi system playing outside one of the houses.

However, I heard and saw nothing of the sort, and nothing else that could explain the presence of the music. The neighbourhood was fast asleep. The locus of the procession's sounds remained about seven metres distant from me, and as I walked northwards, they receded, always keeping the same distance away – but always sounding as if they were approaching. The music had a strange 'floating and flowing' quality; it emanated from where a real procession in the middle of the road would naturally originate, and I could also hear the instruments and vocal harmony coming from further along the road, giving the impression of a long procession. I stood to stop and listen, not far from a farm lodge on the left-hand side of the road, and the procession halted as before, but still sounding as if was coming my way. Eventually, I came to the conclusion I was at a dead end; I wasn't going to find out any more about this 'phantom procession' then and there, so I turned around and walked home. I wondered if it could be a ghostly procession, or a timeslip, I had read about them, as well as eyewitness accounts of railway locomotives, complete with carriages, seen steaming along a disused cutting; the tracks had been lifted long ago.

A day after the event, I told a few friends what I had witnessed, but I could see they thought I was mistaken, and that the real cause was one of those I had already looked for and found no trace of. I'm sure I would disbelieve it too, had anyone told me they'd experienced such a thing. For that reason, I haven't spoken about it to anyone else until recently. When I decided, at last, to write an account of the 'procession', I mentioned it to my two sisters; they listened in silence, but when I had finished, they reacted with the same sceptical response as had my friends all those years ago.

Since then I have researched historic processions in the area and found nothing. It has remained a question mark in the back of my mind ever since. I would like to know whether anyone else has had a similar experience on this stretch of road.

This strange event didn't ruffle me at all; it only piqued my curiosity, because at the time I was becoming used to witnessing paranormal events, and had no problem keeping an open mind as I am sceptical by nature.

Once we encounter the unknown, the uncanny, the paranormal, call it what-you-will, in a way that is certain, with no other possible explanation, we can only echo the famous Sherlock Holmes quote, 'When you have eliminated all which is impossible, then whatever remains, however improbable, must be the truth.' It feels as if there has been a seismic shift deep within your psyche, and you will never see the world in quite the same way again.

As a coda to this event, there are three things I will mention. The first is that each time I was dropped off and walked up the avenue (the avenue runs uphill), it was always between 1.30 a.m. and 3.30 a.m., and on every occasion I saw a petite, thin old lady standing in front of her bungalow about two-thirds of the way up. She wore her long white hair parted in the centre, and was always clad only in the same white cotton nightdress that she wore every time I saw her, no matter what the weather, and she had the most beautiful smile. I always said 'Good night' to her as I passed by. Sometimes I would remember to wish her 'Good morning,' but not once did she reply or respond in any way; she stood always in the same place, always completely motionless, looking down the avenue, smiling her wonderful smile. It was a long time after I had ceased to come home so late that it finally occurred to me that this lady might have been a ghost. I don't have an opinion either way, but I thought it worth including here.

The second thing is that the direction of the 'procession' was towards Leicester, but in the centre of Syston is a crossroads, and a right turn leads towards the Church of St Peter and St Paul, a possible destination for a Christian procession.

Another, very tenuous, possibly pagan, link is the 'Moody Bush', a small standing stone in a field just off an ancient track called 'The Ridgemere', said to be the site of tribal (or village) moots, meetings of the local chiefs or elders; the 'away team' always bringing with them a sod of turf to represent the presence of their 'home turf'. It is situated approximately two kilometres (1.25 miles) distant from the stretch of road where I heard the 'procession', in an east-southeast direction. I include this because in the Domesday Book, Syston is listed as 'Sitestone', and it has been suggested it's from this 'Moody Bush' stone that Syston derives its name.

The A607 starts from Belgrave, Leicester, passing through Syston, Melton Mowbray and Grantham before terminating on the outskirts of Lincoln; it was once the turnpike road from Leicester to Melton and other points northeast, with around two thousand coaches a year using it in Georgian times.

The Séance

Many years ago, before I had even left home to get married to my first husband, I was close to my eldest brother, both in age and nature. We were interested in the same bands, writers, artists and subjects, and we often swapped books and talked into the evenings about the paranormal. My then-boyfriend, who became my husband, had abilities that defied logic, and this was interesting to both myself and my brother.

One evening, we had been discussing the paranormal, and my father and mother - both extremely sceptical - were disputing that such things existed, whereas we were arguing that ghosts and spirits were not only real, but were all around us. Dad was quite scathing until my brother suggested a séance. Having taken part in one the year before, I was reluctant, but Dad was by now curious.

We set it up with handwritten letters and numbers at the dining table. In the interest of being objective, my boyfriend sat out so it was my brother, father, mother and myself taking part. For a while, all we were getting – much to my Dad's satisfaction - was nonsense. I asked the usual questions: 'Is anyone there?' and 'Why are you here?'

Suddenly, the upturned glass took on a different 'feel' - it no longer felt free, but as if it was under some strange control. In answer to my questions we got 'Yes' and 'To talk to Joe' - my father's name. He accused my brother and I of manipulating the glass, but of course, we were doing no such thing.

I asked, 'What is your name?' And the answer staggered my Dad. It was the name of an old style music hall comedian, one who had been great friends with my grandfather and who had died many years before. There was no way we could have known the name - my grandfather had died the year I was ten, and had never mentioned the name in front of his grandchildren, and nor had my father.

Dad visibly blanched - one of the very, very few times I remember my dad being shocked or scared. The atmosphere was electric, and then the glass lifted off the table, despite all four of us trying to stop it rising. At this point, my still sceptical mother rose from the table, grabbed the glass and messed up the letters - she was furious that we would trick my dad in this way, even though we both denied it. Dad was adamant that we could not have known that name, but the spell had been broken, and we stopped.

For many years after, my formally sceptical dad dined out on this story, telling it over and over to everyone - it had really caught his imagination, and in some ways was a blessing as he neared his end, as he firmly believed in an afterlife from that day onward.

My sceptical mother? She remained a sceptic all her life, completely denying any afterlife at all. Quite ironic really, as although she passed nearly fourteen years ago, she likes to make herself known, and indeed I had a visit from her last week (just to tell me off to be honest). Sadly, so far Dad has not come through, although I live in hope.

A Victorian Visitor

In 1963 my family moved to a new house in Basingstoke. Not the most likely location for a haunting, you might think, and for the first few years that we lived there nothing out of the ordinary seems to have happened. But in September 1970, when I was seventeen, I saw a ghost.

I woke in the night to see a young girl standing by my bed. She was aged about twelve, and quite unknown to me, but what was stranger still was her appearance, and what then happened. She was dressed in Victorian clothes, and her hair was tied into two plaits which hung down in front of her shoulders. I had the distinct impression that she was holding a book. Neither she nor I said anything, and as I looked on, she rose upwards, vanishing through the ceiling, displaying her underskirts and buttoned-up boots.

I didn't tell anybody about this, of course, and tried to convince myself that it must have been a dream. Some while later, however, this was to change. Why? I shared my bedroom with my sister, and one night she woke me. She was plainly disturbed, and it took a bit of time to get her to tell me what was wrong. She said that she had seen a girl standing by my bed, dressed like a Victorian, but she thought that she'd been carrying a teddy bear rather than a book. So that's when I told her that I'd seen her about the same time of year the year before. After this, we told Mum, who said that she'd once seen a young girl sitting on our stairs. Who was she?

The Penrhyncoch Phantom

I have only had one brief ghostly experience in my life and it goes as follows. Back in 1991 I had a 50cc motorbike that I used to get to work on. It would not go faster than 30 miles per hour, so was pretty slow. I lived high up in the hills of Wales in a very rural area. It was several miles to get to work.

One misty morning, I was riding my bike to work as usual, and you could see no further than thirty feet in front of you before the view was fully obscured by the mist. I came down into the valley near the first village of my journey, and as I came to pass an old stone bridge there was a woman all dressed in black wearing a headdress (I would say Victorian era clothing), standing centrally at the edge of the bridge looking out over the river, so I couldn't see her face.

As I got within a few feet of her, she turned and looked directly into my eyes with a piercing stare. It sent shivers down my spine, I can tell you. This all happened in a split second, for as soon as she had looked at me I had already passed her by.

She had a gaunt looking middle-aged face, and I couldn't get that stare out of my mind. But when I looked back in my mirror, there was no one there. I proceeded to stop, and physically look around without getting off of my bike. And yet, there was no one there, and also nowhere for her to have hidden, or to have slipped out of view.

Feeling unnerved, I rode off as fast as I could to get away from the area. I never saw her again.

Hauntings at Kenilworth Castle

I've been fortunate enough to work for English Heritage and the National Trust, and spent many years getting to know haunted castles and spooky stately homes.

One of the best parts of working in heritage is learning that most places have not only an official history that we share with the visitors, but also an unofficial folklore passed down through the people who live and work there.

I'll start with some stories from my first job at Kenilworth Castle in Warwickshire, an incredible place with a long history dating back some 900 years. Originating as a medieval fortress, it was subsequently transformed into a Tudor palace before becoming a scenic ruin after the English Civil War. It was also named English Heritage's second spookiest castle (after Bolsover Castle in Derbyshire).

Most of the supernatural activities were confined to the still intact structures of Leicester's gatehouse and the stables. Whilst I was perfectly happy to walk around most of the ruins by myself after dark, the gatehouse was another story. It had an unfriendly presence after dark and, it must be said, often during the daytime.

Visitors and staff reported a strong smell of tobacco smoke or burning in some of the rooms. I was sceptical of this for a while, as I thought maybe someone was having a cheeky ciggie, until one day when I popped downstairs into the basement to wash my hands. As I leaned over the sink (I must add here that the room was windowless) there was suddenly a very strong and unmistakable smell of smoke, as though someone had exhaled a cigarette directly into my face. Then as soon as I noticed it, it was gone again; a pretty bizarre experience.

Supernatural activity seemed to be focused around the bedroom, as well as the staircase with its associated landing and the staff offices. One evening my manager had been working late when she heard footsteps coming down the stairs from the attic. There was a loud bang as though someone had jumped down the last few steps. The latch on the door then flicked up and down, before the heavy fire door slowly creaked open and slammed violently shut again. You will not be surprised to learn that she made a swift exit after this.

For a while we held sleepovers at the castle, where visitors could book to stay overnight in the gatehouse (rather them than me). After serving them breakfast the next morning they sometimes complained that they hadn't slept a wink as 'the staff' had been running and jumping on the stairs all night. We had to break it to them that the only staff member in the building hadn't left the office all night.

The bedroom next to the office had a very heavy atmosphere, and most of the staff didn't like being in there alone. Inside it had an old four-poster bed and a wooden cradle, the latter often seen rocking by itself, and our night security guard told us that it would often set off the motion sensor alarms.

One morning our manager found a tennis ball perfectly balanced on the very edge of the top step next to the bedroom as though it was being held there. She thought one of us might have done it as a prank, but none of us had been upstairs yet. We also found it was impossible to replicate, as whenever we placed the ball in the same place she'd found it, the ball would inevitably roll off the step.

The gatehouse ghosts were rumoured to be a young girl who would ask for her daddy, a dark male figure who had been killed in a sword fight and an old lady who was seen in one of the turret rooms/chapel (although I never heard anything about the old lady in stories amongst the staff). I do know that the chapel room next to the bedroom gave me the heebie jeebies, and I spent as little time in there as possible.

The stables at Kenilworth Castle are impressive, built from a mixture of wattle and daub, as well as stone, and possess a high, wooden vaulted ceiling. The building dates back to 1553 and was built by Robert Dudley's father, John Dudley. Such is the scale of the building that it evokes more of a medieval great hall than somewhere you would stall your horses. These horses would have lived a life of luxury, even compared to most people at the time. Today, it houses the modern tearoom and kitchen at one end, and a museum display at the other.

I have very fond memories of the stables as this is where we held our staff parties after hours and things often got a bit 'merry'. Perhaps this is why I felt the stables had such a welcoming atmosphere. (I won't say it was a 'warm' welcome as the underfloor heating didn't work, and the temperature would often dip below freezing in there in the winter, often with snow blowing in through the gaps in the walls.)

Whereas there was a 'presence' in this building, it never felt as unfriendly or oppressive as the gatehouse often did. However, whoever was acting as tearoom supervisor would always keep the kitchen door to the main stables building locked whenever they were in there alone. Even some of my more sceptical colleagues were prone to secure themselves in this way. This wasn't for security reasons, as the other main doors into the stables would be bolted shut when we weren't open to the public. Instead, this had more to do with the odd things you would catch out of the corner of your eye.

The kitchen itself is housed in what looks like a large wooden box within the cavernous walls of the stables, making it a self-contained unit with a glass panelled door that leads out to the serving counter and dining area in the main stables building. Through this door you could see the entire length of the stables, and almost everyone who worked in the kitchens reported seeing strange shadows and figures moving around when nobody else was present.

I had one of my strangest experiences in the stables, and it's one that I'm still not sure how to explain. We had a coffee machine on the counter and underneath this was a drawer for the used coffee grounds that we'd empty, clean and then put back at the end of the day.

Both my colleague and I clearly remember cleaning the coffee machine as normal and replacing the drawer before we locked up for the evening. We were the last ones in the serving area as we locked up and set the alarm.

The next morning we opened up and again we were the first into the building. We found the drawer from the coffee machine sitting on a table about thirty feet away from the machine. There was just no conceivable reason why it would have ended up there. We laughed it off as a trick played on us by one of the mischievous spirits, perhaps the stable boy who was rumoured to haunt the building.

I did also hear that members of staff and the public had heard or seen ghostly chickens around the stables. I never witnessed the phantom poultry myself, but I can't say I would have been especially terrified if I had. So, it would seem that I'm not a chicken after all.

The Vanishing Hotel

I'm going to tell you about a strange happening some years ago when I went on a touring holiday with my parents. I was sixteen at the time. We had started the long journey home from Scotland, planning to stay in York, but we only got as far as the Borders. It was getting late and was raining, so my dad pulled into a little town – Jedburgh. The first hotel was full so he tried the other one. There was one old boy propping up the bar, and although it was pretty old fashioned, they did at least have a room. Having booked in, the landlady left us to it.

It wasn't exactly impressive: the room was really dusty; there were bugs crawling up the walls; and the nylon sheets needed changing. When we tried to find the landlady, she was nowhere to be seen, and having eventually located the bathroom down the hall, it was in a similarly filthy state, looking like it hadn't been cleaned in years. Still, we decided to suck it up, as it was just the one night after all.

When we went down for breakfast, we were surprised to find that we were the only guests, although there were lots of photos on the walls showing that this had at least once been a thriving place. We left and were soon on our way, giving it no further thought.

On a later holiday we found ourselves in Majorca, and whilst staying at our hotel we got talking to a Yorkshire couple about bad hotels, and we told them about the Swan. By chance their daughter happened to live in Jedburgh, so they asked when we were there. When they learned of the time of our stay they asserted in the most emphatic terms that there was no way we could have stayed there, because it had closed down years before when the owner died.

The Cutthroat Sailor of Corfe

We used to spend a lot time in the county as we had friends who owned a bed and breakfast there. On one occasion we went to a pub in Corfe just below the castle. It was a lovely evening, and the table under the window by the door wasn't taken so we sat there. I was quite young and very much in love with my husband. Suddenly, I felt a sharp pain in my throat and felt as if I couldn't breathe. I put my hands up to my throat and suddenly all the locals in the pub were laughing or murmuring.

One man came over and said, 'We always leave that table unoccupied. A Victorian sailor once caught his sweetheart cheating, and found her at that table with her lover, so he cut her throat. He's still here. He always goes for pretty young brunettes. The minute you sat down there we knew it would happen again.'

Further Publications

If you enjoyed this book, please consider leaving a review or a rating on Amazon. The following titles are available in paperback, and Kindle, exclusively from Amazon:

A Ghost Story Omnibus Volume Two
A Ghost Story Omnibus Volume Three
Curious England: A Guide
Curious England Volume Two
Curious England Volume Three
Uncanny Tales
Anthology: Wry Out West
Upon Barden Moor: An Occult Mystery
Old Crotchet's Return: A Ghost Story

H.E. Bulstrode Online

To keep abreast of my current and future publications, please follow me on your local Amazon store.

Blog: http://www.hebulstrode.co.uk

Facebook: https://www.facebook.com/H.E.Bulstrode

Printed in Great Britain
by Amazon

56678831R00067